FRON-GOCH
and the birth of the IRA

LYN EBENEZER

ISBN: 0-86381-977-X

Cover design: Sion Ilar
Map: Ken Gruffydd

Adapted from the Welsh publication
Y Pair Dadeni, Hanes Gwersyll y Fron-goch (2005)

First published in English 2006 by
Gwasg Carreg Gwalch, 12 Iard yr Orsaf, Llanrwst,
Wales LL26 0EH.
Tel 01492 642031   Fax 01492 641502
e-mail: books@carreg-gwalch.co.uk
website: www.carreg-gwalch.co.uk

4

Contents

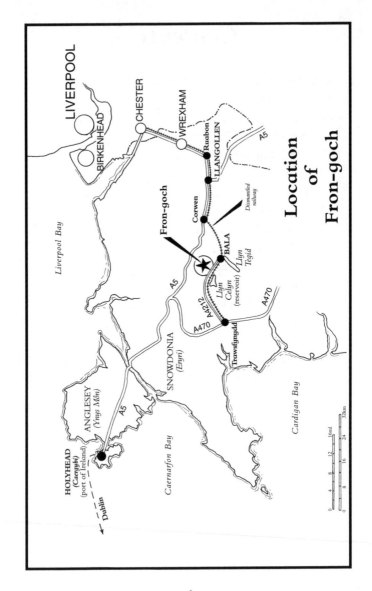

Location of Fron-goch

This book is dedicated
to the memory of
Joe Clarke
(Seosam Ó Cléirigh)
– hero and friend

Author's Note

My interest in Fron-goch Internment Camp began back in Easter 1966, when I attended the fiftieth anniversary commemoration of the Rising in Dublin. Following that visit I repeatedly returned to Dublin and in doing so I met Joe Clarke, who then ran the Irish Book Bureau at 68 Upper O'Connell Street.

Joe was a Fron-goch veteran and a committed Republican who had distinguished himself in the battle of Mount Street Bridge, and it was he who sowed the seed that was to grow into an obsession. I simply wanted to know more and more of the history of the Camp where the leaders of a new Ireland had been trained.

One lesson I learned was that I, as a Welshman, am a member of a nation that treated the Irish just as harshly as did the British in general. We now present ourselves as proud fellow Celts. but some Welsh people were amongst the very worst of those who sought to keep Ireland in shackles. Thankfully, there were other Welsh people, including many of the inhabitants of the Bala area, who treated the Irish internees and their ambitions with compassion and respect.

I do not expect this book to eradicate the blot from the Welsh collective conscience. But as an unashamed Hibernophile, it is my hope that it will at least lighten the stain.

I wrote this book not as a historian but as a working journalist. I also wrote it from a Welsh perspective. More and more Welsh people are eager to learn about Fron-goch and its place not only in a Welsh and Irish context but also in a global context.

I have used the official spelling of Fron-goch, save in circumstances where the place name occurs in quotations.

Lyn Ebenezer
Autumn 2005

Prologue

Easter Monday 1916 dawned brightly in Dublin. The docks lay idle along the Liffey with cargo ships at anchor and the gantries rising silent and still like huge herons above the river. Some inhabitants were still rubbing the sleep from their eyes, while the early risers were determined to be among the first to head for the beaches of Killiney, Dalkey, Bray and Malahide, some on bikes, some travelling by tram. Others, particularly off-duty British soldiers, were heading for the annual Ward Union Point-to-Point horse races at Fairyhouse. One of the horses listed to ride there was named Civil War.

There was another reason for the casual attitude of Dubliners on this fine April morning. It was a Bank Holiday, and those who were sensible were still asleep. But not all Dubliners were sensible on that sunny spring morning. As the sun rose above Howth Head, some 1,200 badly-armed Irish rebels were preparing to take on the might of over 2,500 British soldiers.

In his home at 27 Upper Rutland Street, an assistant at the National Library was up early. The thirty-three-year-old librarian was meant to distribute posters that morning, proclaiming an Irish Republic. At that very moment, the first run of a thousand copies was being printed by Christopher Brady on his ancient Wharfdale press.

Meanwhile, in a safe house near Stephen's Green in Ranelagh, a diminutive, weak and short-sighted man from Rush, County Dublin, was polishing a pistol. He had noticed that the ancient relic was prone to an over-recoil when it was fired. It was this fault in the firearm that would save his life three days later. As he left for the Mount Street area, he had no idea that he would not return for seven months.

At 3 Seafield Road it was work on the stage that paid for

the sustenance of an artistic-looking twenty-year-old. He had little appetite on this particular morning. Usually it was nerves before a first-night performance that would affect his eating habits. Indeed, that very evening he was due to appear at the Abbey Theatre in T. H. Nally's *Spancell of Death*. Instead, in a few hours he would appear on the greatest stage he was ever destined to tread.

In a city centre hotel, two very different men were engaged in quiet discussion with Joseph Plunkett, who was riddled with tuberculosis. Plunkett was to die within eleven days, not from his illness but by firing squad. One of his companions was a dapper ex-farmer from Ferns in County Wexford. But his place on this particular morning, as an officer in the Irish Volunteers, was at the Metropole Hotel between the General Post Office and the river in Sackville Street. The other was a Cork man, an ex-clerk who was young and energetic and walked with a confident, arrogant sway in his gait.

A library assistant, a shop worker, an actor, an ex-farmer and an ex-clerk: five men who would soon be united and tempered by the conflagration of the Easter Rising and who would, in less than two months' time, be re-united in captivity in the hinterland of north Wales, where they would spend between two and seven months. They would be among over eighteen hundred of their fellow Irishmen held together. By the end of the year, Seán T. O'Kelly, Joe Clarke, Arthur Shields, W. J. Brennan-Whitmore and Michael Collins would emerge among the first graduates of Ireland's University of Revolution in Wales: Fron-goch Internment Camp near Bala.

1
A Pram and a Pickfords Van

Opinions vary about which shots were fired first in the Easter Rising, an event that George Bernard Shaw described as a collision between a pram and a Pickfords van. Most historians agree that the first casualty was an unarmed sentry shot dead by members of James Connolly's Irish Citizen Army as they attempted to isolate Dublin Castle soon after noon on Easter Monday. In *Insurrection in Dublin* the author James Stephens, on the other hand, describes how he was witness to what he believed to be one of the first civilian killings of the rebellion – that of an innocent bystander whose handcart or 'lorry' had been commandeered at about 5.00 on Monday evening by Irish Volunteers to form a barricade near Stephen's Green. As the man attempted to retrieve his cart, a Volunteer shot him dead. 'At that moment,' says Stephens, 'the Volunteers were hated.'

The tactics used by the rebels were outmoded and had proved unsuccessful more than a century earlier, when Robert Emmet had attempted a rebellion in 1803. Emmet was a young Protestant who was captured and publicly hanged in Dublin Castle. Sixteen of his men were also executed. His tactics, like Connolly's in 1916, involved taking strategic buildings and holding them against enemy attack.

In a letter to the *Evening Herald* on the 8th of January 1966, Commandant W. J. Brennan-Whitmore, who had been in command of the Volunteers at the head of North Earl Street, wrote that the tactics employed in the 1916 Rising 'were no more elaborate than the surprise seizure of previously selected buildings, fortifying them as best we could, and holding them for as long as possible'.

Past rebellions in Ireland had been easily put down by Crown forces, but what made the leaders of the 1916 Easter Rebellion feel that this one would be different was Britain's involvement in the Great War: many Irish Republicans believed in the slogan 'England's Difficulty is Ireland's Opportunity'. The Irish Home Rule Bill had been outvoted three times – once in the Commons and twice in the House of Lords – and the Great War meant that the Bill was now on hold. But as it seemed inevitable that it would become a reality once the war was over, the Ulster Unionists had taken up arms to defend the Union with the slogan 'Ulster Will Fight, and Ulster will be Right'.

The Republicans had reacted to the Unionists' arming by themselves smuggling weapons into Howth in 1914. Now in 1916 they believed that they were ready to strike. Unfortunately, the Rising was planned and executed in a farcical manner. Firstly, the Irish Volunteers and members of the Irish Citizen Army (the ICA), which had been formed originally to defend workers from strong arm tactics by the constabulary, were told to mobilise on Easter Sunday. The ICA had been created by James Larkin and James Connolly, who were leaders of the General Workers' Union. Connolly was also one of the signatories of the Proclamation of the Republic of Ireland, copies of which were posted all round the city and read to a bemused crowd by its author, Padraig Pearse, from the steps of the General Post Office on Easter Monday. Secondly, a German ship carrying Russian arms intended for the rebels was scuttled near Daunt's Rock off Queenstown (now known as Cobh Harbour). Thirdly, Sir Roger Casement, scholar and diplomat, having failed to raise a battalion from among the captured Irish prisoners of war in Germany, returned on a German submarine and was arrested by the constabulary as he landed, sea-sick and forlorn, in a dinghy on the Kerry coast. Finally, at the last minute, the call to mobilise was cancelled, but the order was ignored by many of the leaders. So, almost entirely confined to Dublin, it began a day late.

The Republicans were outnumbered some two to one, and their cause was a hopeless one from the beginning. The fortified buildings that were taken over in and around the city centre fell one by one. A British anti-submarine vessel, the *Helga*, which sailed up the mouth of the Liffey, virtually destroyed the city centre with shells fired from its three-foot gun. The only surprise was that the insurgents managed to hang on to their positions for six days. The Rising ended on the following Saturday afternoon when Pearse surrendered outside the General Post Office.

Welsh people, whether at home in Wales or among the British soldiers serving in Ireland, were rather puzzled by the action of the thousand or so Republicans who had taken up arms. Wales, like Ireland, had sent more than its share of young men to the trenches of France and Belgium. In fact, some thirty-five thousand Welshmen were to lose their lives in the Great War, and during the Rising Welsh soldiers were among the British troops trying to dislodge the Volunteers and members of the Irish Citizen Army from strategic buildings in Dublin.

Among Welsh people caught up in the chaos were John and Freda Lloyd-Jones. John Lloyd-Jones was Professor of Welsh at the University of Ireland, specialising in early Welsh poetry. The family lived at 129 St Lawrence Road, Clontarf. They were faithful members of Bethel, the little Welsh chapel that was home from home to Welsh exiles in Dublin. Freda spoke to Huw Llewelyn Williams of the events of that fateful Easter Monday. In Williams' book *Wrth Angor yn Nulyn* [At Anchor in Dublin] she describes her experiences:

As was their custom, many of Dublin's residents had gone to the seaside to Howth or Kingston or Dalkey; others had gone to the countryside or to the races. We went to Howth. And we went to catch the train home; but there was no train. We walked home nine miles. As we approached the city we could hear the crackle of guns in the distance. We reached home safely but slept on the floor in fear of bullets flying in through the windows.

The next Sunday there was no service at Bethel. But by the following Sunday it was business as usual.

After the Rising, those who had fought in Easter Week – and many who had not – were herded together and assessed, and the leaders were taken out and executed. These executions of fifteen men, especially that of James Connolly, who had to be tied to his chair before facing the firing squad, did much to change British – and Irish – public opinion. In his book *Internment*, John McGuffin writes:

> With crassness born of indolent arrogance the British turned the rebels into martyrs. The signatories of the Proclamation of the Republic and others, with four notable exceptions, were shot in the stone-breakers' yard in the north-west corner of Kilmainham jail, commandeered by the British in 1914 to accommodate extra troops. The exceptions were Tom Ceannt, shot in Cork; Eamon de Valera and Countess Markievicz who were reprieved, and Sir Roger Casement, who was hanged. The last to be shot were Connolly and McDermott, the one severely wounded, the other a polio victim. Poets and song writers rushed for their pens. The English had done it again.

The fifteen dead leaders could well have been sixteen, as the life of Professor Eóin MacNéill, founder of the Irish Volunteers, was also under threat. Even though he had sought to call off the Rising, he declared himself as responsible as the executed leaders. Indeed, his execution had been seriously considered, and John Redmond, leader of the Irish Parliamentary Party, was moved to beg for MacNéill's life, stressing that he was Ireland's greatest Gaelic scholar. On hearing this, Lloyd George turned to Asquith and said: 'Good God! We mustn't kill a Gaelic scholar – and that's settled it!' MacNéill was therefore tried on the 22nd of May and was sentenced to penal servitude for life at Dartmoor Prison. Lloyd George thereafter took the credit for saving MacNéill's life.

The intervention by Lloyd George was later recalled by Lloyd George's private secretary, Thomas Jones, in his *Whitehall Diary*. Lloyd George is also reported to have said that executing MacNéill would be like executing T. Gwynn Jones, an eminent Welsh poet who, like MacNéill, was a Gaelic scholar. Eventually the executed fifteen became sixteen when Sir Roger Casement was hanged for treason in August 1916.

Over the period of nine days that the leaders were being executed, the other captured Republicans were being questioned and assessed at Richmond Barracks and Kilmainham Jail. A total of 2,519 Republicans were exiled to various prisons in mainland Britain – Knutsford, Wakefield, Wandsworth, Woking, Lewes, Glasgow and Perth. Later, Usk Prison in Wales would also play its part.

Originally, ninety-seven Republicans had been sentenced to be executed, but their sentences were commuted, and they received prison terms ranging from five years to life. During the next few weeks, six hundred and fifty were freed and allowed back to Ireland. The rest, 1,863 prisoners, were held under the Defence of the Realm Act, which meant there were no charges, no court appearances and no pleas.

Some of the men heard rumours that they would be sent to an internment camp. The Isle of Man had been mentioned, as had St Helena, an island nearly two thousand miles off the West African coast, where other enemies of Britain, including Napoleon and Boer soldiers, had been held in exile. Yet another name was mentioned – the strangely named Frogmore, a place that no one had previously heard of. Frogmore turned out to be Fron-goch, where there was an internment camp within the walls of an old whisky distillery. It had been adapted to house German prisoners of war, and such was the urgency of finding accomodation for so many Republican internees that some sick German prisoners still remained when the first Irish internees arrived. Across the road from the distillery, a second camp made up of wooden huts was busily being prepared.

The first three of what would become a prison population of 1,863 men arrived on Friday the 9th of June. Thereafter, prisoners arrived at regular intervals. Those who were sent to Fron-goch were deemed to be the least dangerous of the 'Shinners' who had dared to tweak Britannia's skirt. 'Shinners' was a derogatory name used to describe members of the Republican Party, Sinn Féin, whose name means 'Ourselves Alone'. Indeed, many of these not only posed little danger, but were quite innocent.

Those who were held at Fron-goch were, therefore, a mixture of men, some of whom had proved themselves in the Easter Rebellion and some of whom had played no part at all. Among the former were Richard Mulcahy, Dick McKee and Michael Collins. The forcing house that was Fron-goch would make them the architects of a new Irish army. Others had played smaller parts but had, nevertheless, been participants in an event that had shaken the world. Of the stretcher bearers who had carried the injured James Connolly from the General Post Office, three were at Fron-goch. So were two men who had raised the flags of freedom over the Post Office. The bugler who had called out Connolly's soldiers at 11.30 on Easter Monday was there, as was the actor who should have been treading the boards in the Abbey Theatre on that fateful day. Two of the prisoners had brothers executed following the Rising. As many as six would become members of Michael Collins' feared hit-squad, the Twelve Apostles, while dozens would become TDs, Members of the Irish Parliament.

One prisoner who had not fired a single shot was Cathal O'Shannon, the man who had been Connolly's representative in Belfast. He had hitch-hiked down to Dublin and knocked on a door of the General Post Office on the Tuesday, and had introduced himself. He was sent packing. The place was full and all the sandwiches had been eaten, so he was advised to find lodgings until it was all over. This he did, but within weeks his lodgings would be at Fron-goch.

Jim Mooney, who lived at Seville Place, and who had lived for a while in Wales, had been at the Fairyhouse Races when he had heard rumours of shootings in Dublin city centre. When he arrived at the General Post Office, he was ordered to report to his unit in Stephen's Green. There he was sent back to the GPO where he was informed that his unit was now in Jacob's Factory. When he reported back to the GPO he was sent home to fetch his arms and ammunition, and ordered to return. He was given the special password – 'O'Donnell Abu' – but when he finally returned, a Glaswegian guard with the Volunteers could not understand him and refused him entry. Mooney was on the brink of giving up when someone in authority recognised him and allowed him in. Soon he would be back in Wales for the second time in his life – in Fron-goch.

One internee, Michael McInerney, was lucky to make it to Fron-goch at all. On Good Friday, he had been one of five men who had been despatched to Caherciveen to contact a German ship, the *Aud*, which had a cargo of Russian arms for the Volunteers. At Ballykissane near Killorglin the car they were in plunged into the river Laune. Three were drowned and McInerney, the driver, was arrested. When he was brought before the court he was asked why he was there. His answer was: 'Because I'm alive.'

The reception that the Irish prisoners met in the Welsh

community of Fron-goch, where they would spend between two and seven months, would have been strongly influenced by the Welsh press, which largely followed the British line. On the 29th of April, however, *The Celt and The London Welshman* rather unexpectedly blamed 'our slackness in the supervision of arms' for causing the Rising. 'The fact is that Ireland has only just been saved from a revolution – not from the Sinn Féin crowd but from "the loyal" patriots of Ulster', the writer observed.

By the following week, however, a correspondent calling himself 'Onlooker' was firmly back in line:

> The end of the Irish Republic came very sudden. It was a disastrous affair from every point of view. As an attempt to overthrow English rule in Ireland it was a mere fiasco, because the nation as a whole did not take any part in the rising. As an organised revolt it was of a purely local character, and no person of influence and position could be found to direct its operations. The whole crowd of agitators were a set of irresponsible fanatics without policy, without ideas and without a spark of practicality.

A Welsh language article in the same issue, however, was reluctant to condemn Sinn Féin, but rather commended its zeal and doughtiness, observing that the leaders knew very well that influential authority was needed before the English would offer a shred of freedom to the Irish. It implied, in fact, that force was the only way. Now that the rebels had been defeated, the subject to be tackled next was how to behave properly towards the hundreds of these men who had been taken into custody.

The article proposed that dealing with them in the same way as de Wet and his pettish party in South Africa had been dealt with would offer the hope that the whole affair would soon be forgotten, but if some were made martyrs, and the leaders received their deserved punishment, this would only add to the evil, which would make more enemies for years to come.

Another Welsh language article in the same paper on the 20th of May went even further. It accused the English of not understanding the Irish problem. Somehow or other, wrote the correspondent, our English neighbours did not believe that patriotism and nationalism existed beyond the borders of their own small country. The Irishman, however, like the Welshman who gave precedence to his own nation, was immediately seen as a traitor. The author continued:

> If the rising in Dublin the other week has been a bitter failure, it must be admitted that the spirit of resistance has not been completely eradicated from the Irish circle.

Indeed, the author went as far as to say that Sinn Féin members, who had sworn to refuse all things English and were ready to sacrifice comfort, health and wealth in order to achieve their goal, had not acted impetuously. In his opinion, the members were much more honest in their beliefs and much more loyal to their land than the arrogant English who filled the London streets with khaki. Indeed Sinn Féin had not ever meant to be a militant movement – it had been Sir Edward Carson who had brought the devil into the circle (Carson was the leader of the Ulster Unionists, a staunch opponent of Home Rule, and was notorious as the prosecutor in the Oscar Wilde trial).

Such sentiments as those found in *The Celt and The London Welshman* were uncommon within Welsh communities. What made these even more unexpected was the fact that they were published in a newspaper boasting a circulation of fifty thousand, which was also read by Welsh people in the English capital.

But what of the mainstream English – and Welsh – press? *The Times*, as was expected, saw the Rising as a German Plot and the 'most sensational domestic incident which the war has produced'. There was no doubt that Sinn Féin had been in league with the enemy, its editorial commented. The Chief Secretary, Birrell – described as 'complaisant and senile' – was made the scapegoat. *The Times* again blamed the 'Irish tumult' on 'German intrigue and bribery, resembling German plots to stir up Japan and Mexico against the United States'. It added with much pleasure on the 4th of May that the friends of efficient government would hear with a measure of satisfaction the announcement that three of the leading rebels had been executed.

The daily press in Wales tended to follow the opinion of the English-based newspapers. The Wales edition of the *Liverpool Daily Post and Mercury* headlined the first news of the Rising as 'Irish Coast Sensation'. Here the 'German Plot' was encapsulated in a character assassination of Casement, which entailed allegations about his time in Germany. While recruiting in Germany, the newspaper claimed, he had been attacked in a POW camp by unarmed Irish prisoners who were incensed by his appeal for them to join the German army. Only the intervention of armed German sentries, claimed the *Post*, had saved the 'traitor' from injury.

In its editorial, the paper called for the revolt to be 'sternly and mercilessly repressed by all the resources at the command of the Government'. It welcomed the Government's opportunity 'of making a clean sweep of the disloyal element which has been a canker at the heart of the community'.

The Wales edition of the *Manchester Guardian,* on the other hand, was far more conciliatory, observing: 'The only people who can effectively maintain order are the Irish themselves and their leaders in the Irish Parliamentary party.' In its editorial on the 13th of May it described the Rising as 'one of the most fantastic and hopeless revolts known to history'. Following the last two executions – those of Connolly and Seán MacDiarmada – it stated that the act had been carried out as a tribute to that sense of symmetry which stands in the place of justice in times of rebellion and repression....Would the bones of any of the men previously executed have cried out had these two been spared? We can only trust that these will be the last, that if there are common murderers to be tried they will be brought before a civil court, and that a definite end will now be put to the disposal of men's lives by military courts.

The newspapers, in the main – discounting the *Guardian* – echoed the feelings of British people. *The Western Mail*, published in Cardiff, bracketed the Rising with the simultaneous German attack by Zeppelins and warships on the east coast of England. The Rising itself was described as 'a serious disturbance'. The writer remarked:

The Germans have always counted upon armed insurrection in Ireland. They have striven to provoke it from the outbreak of the war, and at last they have succeeded in getting their dupes to indulge in an insane rising.... It is evidently the result of a carefully arranged plot, concocted between the Irish traitors and their German confederates.

In Wales itself there were very few supporting voices for the Rebels. Even though there was some backing from trade unionists for the ideals of Larkin and Connolly, Captain Jack White paid a heavy price when he left Dublin for Wales immediately after Easter Week to seek support from the miners. White had fought against the British in the Boer War, and had trained the Irish Citizen Army. His hope was that miners in the south Wales valleys would strike in protest against the likely executions of the leaders, and he believed that Connolly's plight in particular would evoke sympathy.

A much-respected soldier and the son of Field Marshall

George White of Ladysmith, White was arrested and charged. The charges were that on the 8th of May at Trecynon – four days before Connolly was executed – he had unlawfully spread reports and made statements likely to cause disaffection to His Majesty and likely to prejudice recruiting, and that he had unlawfully in his possession documents that would be likely to arouse disaffection. In short, he was accused of contravening the Defence of the Realm Act, or DORA.

White was taken by train from Swansea to Aberdare Police Court where, according to the *Aberdare Leader* of the 27th of May, a large crowd had gathered that included his wife and his mother. The court was told that White had a history of involvement with labour troubles in Dublin, as he had played an active part in the Transport Strike of 1913. His activities had included training the Irish Citizen Army and he was known to have been in contact with James Larkin, Sir Roger Casement, Countess Markievicz, James Connolly, James Plunkett, Sheehy Skeffington 'and others who figured so disastrously in recent events in Dublin'.

According to local lawyer Ivor Parry, who opened the prosecution, White had come to Wales 'with the avowed object of inducing the miners to come out on strike to compel the Government to show leniency to the leaders of the rebellious outbreak in Ireland'.

A prosecution witness, David Tyssul Davies of Trecynon, testified that White had told him that the object of his visit 'was to organise the south Wales miners to act with a view to preventing Jim Connolly being executed'. Davies went further, however, and stated that the accused had told him that he hoped Germany would win the war.

White dismissed Davies' testimony as 'a tissue of falsehoods', but the Stipendiary Magistrate, after noting that the state of affairs in Ireland was very grave, accused White of 'coming over to sow the seeds of sedition in a district which had nothing to do with the grievances of Ireland, either real or imagined'. At a time when the rebellion had been quelled and tranquillity was about to be restored, White was found guilty on two counts, and was given two jail sentences of three months, to run concurrently.

In his essay 'The Black Hand: 1916 and Irish Republican Prisoners in North Wales', Jon Parry states:

> In 1916 Wales was a loyal pillar of the British Empire: its mines were fuelling the war effort and its greatest son, Lloyd George would soon be in the seat of power as prime minister. Although its old, Edwardian confidence was under threat from the strain of war and the modernising of society, it was staunchly unionist in terms of its position within the United Kingdom. Preparations for Welsh Home Rule were in hand but they were becoming increasingly redundant.

Jon Parry claims that some of the leaders of political and industrial labour in Wales had become part of the wartime government:

> They, too, had little sympathy with those who had rebelled against the Crown. In his capacity as a junior minister at the Home Office, William Brace, one of the pioneering leaders of the South Wales Miners' Federation and now turned elegant parliamentarian, had the task of reporting on and defending the conditions in Frongoch camp to the House of Commons. Welsh Labour MPs may have joined in with Arthur Henderson when he allegedly applauded the execution of the Rising's leaders, including James Connolly. Other men with personal or commercial Welsh connections would one day be trying to maintain British authority from Dublin Castle.

One of those at Dublin Castle who had Welsh connections was Sir Hamar Greenwood (he was of Welsh parentage). Greenwood oversaw the Black and Tans and the Auxiliaries, British 'police cadets' – a misnomer if there ever was one - who later operated outside the law during the War of Independence between 1919 and 1921. There was, therefore, not much comradeship with the Irish among the Welsh.

However, there was one notable exception, although his practical support was a year late – Arthur Horner, who was later to become the first Communist to be made President of the South Wales Miners' Federation, and who subsequently served as General Secretary of the National Union of Mineworkers between 1946 and 1959.

Horner supported the Easter Rebellion and was both saddened and infuriated by the execution of James Connolly. In his autobiography, *Incorrigible Rebel*, he writes:

> I had refused to join the armed forces to fight the Germans, because I saw in the coal owners and the Government that supported them a nearer enemy than the Kaiser, but I had smuggled away to Ireland to fight in Connolly's Citizen Army because I believed that the Irish were the only people waging a real war for freedom.

Horner enlisted in the ICA in 1917 under an assumed name – that of a dead man, Jack O'Brien, from County Longford – and was offered work as a window cleaner. When told that he would be expected to stand on window sills he went back to Citizen Hall and said:

> I don't mind being killed for Ireland's freedom, but I'm not having someone write home to the Welsh miners telling them that Arthur Horner was killed cleaning windows at sixpence a time.

In *Incorrigible Rebel,* Horner describes how he practiced in the hills around Dublin during weekends and evenings but never took part in a pitched battle. He lived in Grove Park overlooking Portobello Barracks and could see the English soldiers drilling in the courtyard. He liked to think of himself as having done what the Resistance later did during the Second World War. He described himself singing rebel songs, among them 'Wrap the Green Flag Round Me, Boys'. Little did he realise that the song had been written by a Fron-goch internee.

After some eighteen months in exile, Horner was longing to see his wife and child again and he risked returning home. He was arrested at Holyhead where locals thought he was a German spy. In January 1919 he was dishonourably discharged from an army he had never joined, and was jailed for two years with hard labour.

It is difficult to know how much romanticism is involved in Horner's account. He wrote, for instance, that eleven hundred members of the Irish Citizen Army had turned out during Easter Week. In *The History of the Irish Citizen Army,* R. M. Fox lists a hundred and sixty two names of the ICA participants, twenty-six of them women and ten of them boys. The true figure is perhaps nearer two hundred and twenty, of which nine were killed in the fighting, including fifteen-year-old Charlie Darcy, while James Connolly and Michael Mallin were executed.

In addition to Arthur Horner, one of the very few Welshmen to come out openly in favour of the action taken by Republicans during Easter Week was D. J. Williams. There were a few prominent Welsh scholars, poets and historians who expressed support for the Rising after the fact, but D. J. Williams voiced support at the time.

Williams, or 'DJ' as he was affectionately known, would become one of Wales' most ardent nationalists. Later on, in

1936, he and two fellow activists were jailed for their part in an arson attempt on an RAF bombing school at Penyberth near Pwllheli, which had been built in the face of almost total opposition in Wales. Both of his companions – Lewis Valentine, a pacifist who had served as a stretcher bearer in Ireland, and Saunders Lewis, founder of Plaid Cymru (the Welsh Nationalist Party, now known as The Party of Wales) – had also been prominent in their support for the Irish cause. In November 1920, Valentine, who became a minister of religion, led a party of students who paid homage to the dead hunger-striker Terence MacSwiney as his body was taken by train from London through Bangor railway station to Holyhead. He also led a protest at University College Bangor against the execution of eighteen-year-old Kevin Barry, who was hanged in 1920. Barry was arrested during an ambush that led to the death of three British soldiers, although he himself was not directly responsible for any of the deaths.

Saunders Lewis was an admirer of the educational policies of Padraig Pearse, especially his plans for St Enda, which provided Irish education for Irish pupils. While he was attracted by Sinn Féin's policy of gaining independence through local government rather than through Whitehall, Lewis believed in retaining the Royal connection. He also abhorred Eamon de Valera. When it was suggested that de Valera be invited to Plaid Cymru's first Summer School at Machynlleth in 1926, Lewis utterly opposed the invitation, and instead invited Fine Gael deputy and Dáil member Kevin O'Shiel, who had been Michael Collins' legal advisor and close friend. Lewis had met de Valera and did not like him. He described him as having a mind that was muddled, sottish, windy and disorganised, bereft of philosophy and definite ideas; a man rather full of fruitless and dishonest rhetoric.

At the time of the Rising, D. J. Williams was a student at Oxford, and he wrote for *Y Wawr* [The Dawn], the Welsh language student magazine at the University College of Wales, Aberystwyth. His article 'Y Tri Hyn' [These Three], which was written within days of the Rising, looked at Sinn Féin, the Germans and conscientious objectors. Williams questioned how any true Welshman could not sympathise completely with the plight of the Irish:

> Our government can kill and destroy the Irishman. He cannot be placed with his back against the wall and a bullet shot through his brain and left forgotten. The spirit of a nation conquered through violence is as immortal as the spirit of freedom in a man's heart. The only enemy that can conquer him is the moral corruption that can destroy from within. Give to Ireland a free government free from the English according to centuries of aspirations, and we prophesise for it, in the light of the present awakening, a flourishing period of service to the nations of the world. Trample on it further and Vesuvius will shudder once more.

Williams went on to suggest, ironically, that the warring Sinn Féin surely had no message for him and his readership, the imperial and loyal Welsh:

> Did not every blessing and goodness that the good Lord think we needed come through patient and prayer-like expectations from the Imperial Government? If needs be that we should be meek and servile occasionally, and be prepared to bend the knee to the god of Empire when asked to do so, there is something grand, after all, in fawning to the great, and it always pays for us to be good little children.... Were we, the Welsh, possessed of a third of the courage and unquenchable flame of the Irish in their fight for freedom, the thorough sincerity and the unshakeable quality of the Germans as well as the moral strength of the conscientious objectors, we would have the ability to move the world.

Such words did not go down at all well in Liberal Wales. One of the strongest objectors was the educationalist, historian and author Owen M. Edwards, who was later to be knighted for his services to Welsh education and culture. In his monthly magazine *Cymru* [Wales] he attacked both Williams' article and those who were behind the Rising. While praising John Redmond, leader of the Irish Parliamentary Party, he described the Volunteers as a motley collection of those who were motivated by a hatred of the English, which was fuelled by memories of the past, and a faction of 'uncompromising labourites'. The one side was self-sacrificial, poetic and extremely religious, while the other side was selfish, practical and self-interested. His message was that the English of the day were not the same as oppressors of earlier days.

In the August issue of his magazine, Edwards directly attacked the views of D. J. Williams. Among the three factions Williams had praised – the German, the Sinn Féiner and the conscientious objector – were some, he alleged, whose utterances could only be described as obvious treason. A later article by Williams on the conduct of Britain in the Great War was banned and *Y Wawr* was forced to close.

After the Rising, Williams' theoretical interest in Sinn Féin took a practical turn. He visited Cork in 1920, where he befriended one of the lawyers involved in the inquest into the murder of the city's Lord Mayor, Tomás MacCurtain, who had been killed by the constabulary. This paved the way for him to meet Sinn Féin leaders in Dublin following a clandestine meeting held above a coal merchant's shop in the city. There he spoke to Arthur Griffith and also saw Michael Collins.

Taken together, it is clear that there was, therefore, both some hypothetical and practical support for the rebels among Welsh intellectuals, although mostly in retrospect.

29

There were also Welsh casualties, whose identities have been ignored in accounts of the events of Easter Week. At least two Welsh soldiers lost their lives during the Rising – Private W. Edgar Moy and James T. Wynford Llewellyn. W. Edgar Moy was described by *The Celt and The London Welshman* as 'a young and bright Welshman'. He was the son of Annie James and Edgar Griffith James, who was deputy-manager of the Caerau Colliery, Maesteg. He was fatally wounded as he marched with eighty-four of his comrades towards the city centre on that Easter Monday. A member of the Glamorgan Yeomanry, he had enlisted at Bridgend, and was buried in the Welsh plot in Glasnevin Cemetery. At the Nantyffyllon Eisteddfod held during the same week, the audience stood in silent tribute in memory of the eighteen-year-old man.

T. Wynford Llewellyn, the other soldier who was killed, was named in the *Haverfordwest and Milford Haven Telegraph*. He was from Llanstadwel near Neyland, and had enlisted in the Pembrokeshire Yeomanry at Haverfordwest. Private Llewellyn was seventeen years old when he was shot on the 29th of April, the last day of the Rising, and he was buried at the Grangegorman British Military Cemetery at Blackhorse Avenue near Phoenix Park in Dublin.

The Sinn Féin Rebellion Handbook names among the dead a third Welshman, a man with the surname James, from Pembroke. However, the Commonwealth Graves Commission does not record anyone with that surname as having been killed in Dublin at the time.

Four Welshmen are listed in the *Rebellion Handbook* as having been among the wounded, three of them members of the Yeomanry: H. Asbury, from Hope, Flint; T. Jones, from Swansea; R. D. Richards, from Oswestry, and from Pengam a W. Addis, who was a member of the Lancers. *The Haverfordwest and Milford Haven Telegraph* also names George Llewellyn, from Neyland.

Other Welsh soldiers who were involved proved luckier. In the *South Wales Evening Post* on the 16th of May it was reported that Corporal H. L. Morgan from Thornhill in Clydach narrowly escaped with his life. He was among ten other British soldiers captured by a group of Volunteers and put before a firing squad. In a letter to his father, which is quoted in the newspaper, Morgan describes how a Volunteer Captain with whom he was friendly was informed of the impending executions by a young lad he knew, who went running with the message. The Captain arrived just in time to prevent the shootings.

The South Wales Evening Post on the 12th of May mentions Lieutenant T. D. Thomas, who was a member of the Welsh Regiment on holiday in Dublin during that Easter week. On the outbreak of the Rising, he immediately joined the Royal Inniskillins and fought in Sackville Street (later renamed O'Connell Street) in the vicinity of the Post Office.

Accounts of the events of Easter Week are now a blend of fact and fiction, of reality and much mythology. Indeed Celtic mythology could have played a part in one of the central events. Karl Spindler, the Captain of the ship the *Aud*, which was to have brought arms to the Republicans, had been briefed to use code words relating to Celtic myths. It is possible that Roger Casement himself, with his love of tales of chivalry, was responsible for choosing the code words, but it is more likely that the code words were chosen by the leader of the Volunteers Eóin MacNéill, who was an eminent Celtic scholar. The orders, however, became redundant, as the *Aud* had no radio. The signal that the arms were on their way was 'Finn'. The code word for signalling the sight of an approaching submarine off the Irish coast was 'Aisling', and the word 'Bran' was to be used if any untoward event should occur.

'Finn', of course, was Fionn mac Cumhail or Finn Mac

Cool, who was the great leader of the Fianna, the ancient Irish military elite formed in 300 BC to guard the High King. 'Aisling' or 'Ashling' is found in Irish and Scottish myths, and means 'dream' or 'vision'. Bran appears in both Irish and Welsh mythology. In Irish he is found in 'The Voyage of Bran' in the Red Branch, which was first written down in the eighth century. In the collection of Welsh folk-tales called *The Mabinogi,* which go back some thousand years, Bran, or Bendeigeidfran, was a Welsh giant who led a raid across the sea to Ireland to free his sister Branwen who was being held captive. Bran was captured and beheaded. The head, placed to face France, went on actively directing events and guarded 'The Isle of the Mighty' [Ynys y Cedyrn], or Britain, against invasion.

In the story of Bran, the slain Irish soldiers were thrown into the Cauldron of Rebirth in which they came to life again, although without the power of speech. Seven centuries after the tale of Branwen in Irish exile was written, almost two thousand Irish men would be exiled in Wales. There, Fron-goch would be their Cauldron of Rebirth, in which many of them would rediscover and regain their native tongue.

Among those exiles was Desmond Ryan, a man destined to be a writer. Ryan had been a pupil of Padraig Pearse at St Enda and had fought at the Post Office in Dublin. In his book, *Michael Collins and the Invisible Army*, he describes the hotchpotch nature of the men thrown together by fate and locked in together by British justice:

> All Ireland was there, a strange new Ireland reborn in the Easter fires, leaderless, restless, but dimly aware that nothing would be again as of old. Hundreds of men with wrinkles round the eyes of all, an easy strained expression, watching the iron gate . . . All Ireland listens, every grade and every type of Ireland, urban, rural, exiled, home-staying, sane,

1. The author with Joe Clarke in Dublin at the end of the sixties. Joe was involved in the Battle of Mount Street Bridge and spent seven months in Fron-goch.

2. W.J. Brennan-Whitmore as he appeared in the early seventies when the author met him.

3. The author with the legendary Tom Barry in Cork City in 1979. Tom was incarcerated in Kilmainham Jail when Collins was killed.

4. A poster urging voters to support the Liberal candidate David Williams in the Screw Election of 1859.

5. Goscombe John's sculpture of Tom Ellis MP erected in Bala's main street in 1903.

6. R. J. Lloyd Price in his favourite environment on his Game Farm.

7. A portrait of R. J. Lloyd Price which hangs today at Rhiwlas Mansion.

8. A portrait of the racehorse Bendigo,
who at one point saved Lloyd Price from ruin.

9. The Welsh whisky distillery at Fron-goch when it was operating.

10. A poster extolling the virtue of Welsh whisky distilled in Fron-goch.

11. A poster advertising the Welsh Whisky portraying Mrs Lloyd Price in a Welsh costume.

12. Members of the Zig-zag Club, a crew of eccentrics formed by R. J. Lloyd Price who stands second from the left in the back row. He appointed one of his dogs as secretary.

13. *The distillery staff when production of Welsh whisky was at its height.*

14. *The whisky train ready to transport a load of Welsh whisky from Fron-goch station.*

15. *James Connolly's men, the Irish Citizen Army outside Liberty Hall, once a hotel kept by a Welsh family.*

16. *Liberty Hall today, on the same site as the original building.*

17. *Liberty Hall is still the headquarters of the workers' union as it was in 1916.*

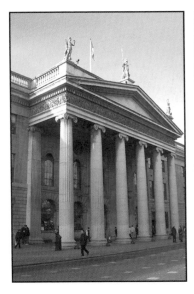

18. & 19.
*The GPO on O'Connell Street (left)
and the sign above the door.*

20. *A painting of the signing of the
Proclamation portraying some of the
leaders of the Rising.*

21. *The rebel flag is raised. Two men
who raised Republican flags above the
GPO were interned in Fron-goch.*

22. *A portrait of Michael Collins defending the Post Office in the Rising.*

23. *Some of the damage caused by the shelling around the Post Office.*

24. *Some of the rifles used by Volunteers in the Rising. They may be seen at the National Museum.*

25. *The Four Courts on the Liffey where the Civil War was triggered.*

26. The old Royal Barracks, today Collins Barracks, now holding some of the National Museum archives.

27. A copy of the rebel flag kept at the National Museum in Dublin.

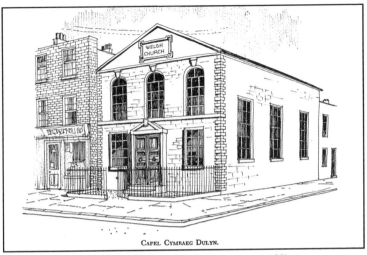

CAPEL CYMRAEG DULYN.

*28. The Welsh Chapel in Talbot Street, Dublin
where explosives and ammunition were once found.*

*29. Today the Welsh Chapel houses
gambling machines.*

*30. Professor J. Lloyd-Jones,
who witnessed the Rising.*

31. *Kilmainham Gaol's main doorway. Today the prison is a museum.*

32. *The 1916 corridor where the leaders of the Rising were held.*

33. *Padraig Pearse's cell door. From here he was taken to his death.*

34. *Political graffiti in Kilmainham Gaol. The name 'M. Collins' was scratched by a guard outside the window of de Valera's cell during the Civil War. Collins was never held there.*

35. The cross marks the spot where the leaders were shot in the Stonebreakers' Yard.

36. The Irish tricolour flies above a place of remembrance.

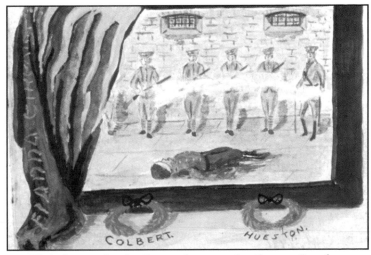

37. A picture painted at Fron-goch representing the execution of one of the leaders.

38. A rare photograph of Michael Collins.

39. German prisoners being counted outside Fron-goch's South Camp.

40. *Captain John McBride being escorted to captivity.*
He was one of fifteen men executed.

41. *Captured rebels being herded to North Wall*
and the cattle ship Slieve Bloom.

THE IRISH MAIL BOATS   HOLYHEAD STATION

42. The port of Holyhead as it appeared some ten years after the rebels of 1916 were landed there.

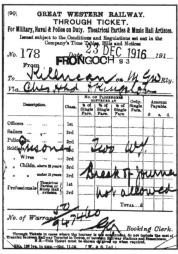

43. A train permit allowing an internee to travel from Fron-goch station.

44. A harp carved in Fron-goch from a cattle bone.

45. Internees being searched in the South Camp's main compound.

46. A crew of kilted Scottish soldiers guarding the internees.

mad, non-descript, in the diverse garbs of Ireland, with Ireland's many accents . . .

Beneath the routine of the camp, Ryan writes, a ferment worked:

Harding felt it as he listened in his bunk to all the actions and reactions of the Five Days, told again in the plain speech of the people, vivid, Rabelaisian, tragic. Murmur after murmur, question after question, story after story . . .

This was the beginning of the University of Fron-goch.

2
Welsh Mountain Dew

The people of Cwm Celyn, where Fron-goch stands, are still proud of the good relationship that existed between their forebears and the Irish internees. While the Welsh in general were antagonistic towards the Irish insurgents in Dublin, there was a benign relationship between the internees and the residents of the Bala area, many of whom worked in a civilian capacity in the camp.

In 1916 Cwm Celyn was a community of small farmers who scraped a living on mainly poor land. They were all tenants of the local Big House, Rhiwlas, and were almost one hundred percent Welsh speaking, a fact that caused no little surprise to the internees.

One of those tenants, Davies of Fedw'r Gog, is still celebrated in the area as the inventor of the military tank. Finding it difficult to transport heavy loads over some of his boggier fields, he built tracks to be placed over his wagon wheels. Local tradition tells that a dastardly Captain from the Fron-goch camp stole his invention and passed it on to the British military.

Among the Irish internees, those from rural areas of Ireland would not have felt out of place in the wilds of Meirionnydd. Michael Collins in particular might have appreciated the similarities between West Cork and Cwm Celyn. Not only were the two locations similar in their topography, but they had also suffered the injustice of unscrupulous landlords. As a child in West Cork, Collins would have witnessed attempts by the Irish Land League to unite tenant farmers and to defend those threatened with eviction. Tenants in the Bala area had witnessed similar struggles. Indeed, a meeting of the Land

League addressed by Michael Davitt, a leading Land War activist who became MP for Mayo, was held at nearby Blaenau Ffestiniog in 1885. Some twenty-five years before, Richard Watkin Price of Rhiwlas evicted tenants who had voted in the 1859 election against his friend and associate, the Tory candidate.

Like generations of Irish people, the residents of the Bala area were also familiar with the effects of emigration. In 1862, a colony of seventeen Quaker families from the area fled to Pennsylvania in search of religious freedom, and it was the Bala minister Michael D. Jones who was instrumental in the founding of the Welsh colony in Patagonia in 1886.

Despite a common experience and struggle, there were obvious differences between the background of the local people and that of the internees. The main difference was one of religion: while the internees, almost to a man, were Catholics, the Bala area was a stronghold of nonconformity. It was at Bala that the influential Welsh Methodist Thomas Charles (1755-1814) established his own press to help spread the Word and teach the common people to read. He promoted the Sunday School movement and Bible readings. Such was his influence that queues of people would form to buy bibles at Bala. One young girl, Mary Jones, became a legend after she walked fifty miles barefoot to collect a bible.

However, although it was a stronghold of nonconformity, the religion practised by the people of the area near Fron-goch differed from this mainstream. A streak of stubborn independence ran through it, and this is probably why, in the very heart of such a hotbed of Methodism, Richard John Lloyd Price was permitted in 1889 to establish the whisky distillery that would later become part of the Fron-goch internment camp.

This R. J. Lloyd Price was the grandson of the R. W. Price who had evicted tenants in 1859, and he was the successor as squire of Rhiwlas. It was a wager made by the young squire that led to the name Fron-goch later becoming forever entwined with the history of the Irish Republic. In 1887, this landowner, huntsman, innovator and eccentric was engaged in banter with his friend, Robert Willis, while they attended sheep-dog trials at Hyde Park in London. Whisky was mentioned, and someone asked why was there no Welsh whisky – after all, 'Wales' and 'whisky' shared the same initial, and why should the Welsh not produce a golden liquid as good as that produced by the Scots and the Irish? The seed was sown, and within two years Welsh whisky was flowing into casks and bottles in a new distillery built on the banks of the Tryweryn river.

R. J. Lloyd Price was among the most inventive and innovative characters in Wales in that period. Quixotic and pioneering, and an excessive lover of horses and dogs, he could trace his ancestors back to Marchweithian, the founder of the eleventh of the tribal high orders in Wales. Another of his predecessors, Sir Rhys ap Meredydd, or 'Rhys the Great', had led the men of Hiraethog to Bosworth Field where, following the fall of William Brandon, Henry Tudor's standard bearer, he had raised the Welsh Dragon.

It was Rhys's grandson, Cadwaladr Price, who founded the aristocracy of the Rhiwlas Estate, where the Price family still live. Cadwaladr's brother was Dr Ellis Price, or the 'Red Doctor', a dubious character who was described by traveller and author Thomas Pennant as 'the greatest of our knaves – the most dreaded oppressor in his neighbourhood'. Another member of the dynasty was Thomas Prys of Plas Iolyn, who was reputed to be the first man to smoke openly on the streets of London.

By 1840, the Rhiwlas Estate was one of only five in Meirionnydd with holdings over the ten thousand acre minimum that a landowner needed to possess in order to qualify as a nobleman. The Returns of Owners of Land in 1873 lists Rhiwlas as an estate of 17,717 acres, which brought in an annual rent of £9,386. By 1890 the rental income had risen to £13,000, with an additional £3,000 raised through shooting rents.

R. J. Lloyd Price inherited in 1864 and it was his dream to turn his country estate into a game farm that could compete with the largest in Britain. Einion Wyn Thomas, Archivist at the University College of Wales Bangor describes his activities in detail in an unpublished lecture. According to him, Lloyd Price planted sixty acres of copse to shelter pheasant, and created three huge rabbit warrens – the largest on Glwysan, or 'Eglwys Ann', on land measuring three hundred and fifty acres. On the 7th of October 1885, ten hunters shot over five thousand rabbits there. Breeding grounds were also laid down for the game birds, and the estate produced a special feed called the Rhiwlas Game Meal.

The Rhiwlas Game Farm, which covered over twenty thousand acres, was established in 1880, and was advertised as the oldest and largest in Wales. Among the produce listed were partridge and pheasant eggs. Keepers who collected the eggs were entertained at the Goat Hotel in Bala. Hunters paid between £250 and £300 per season for shooting rights. There were five shooting ranges on the surrounding mountains, and the neighbouring Rhiwaedog Mansion became the Rhiwaedog Sporting Hotel.

Lloyd Price employed numerous keepers and built cottages for them at Cwm, Pant-glas, Brynbabon and at Rhiwlas itself. Baskets full of pheasant and rabbits were carted to the railway station at Bala to be transported to wholesalers in England, and the annual shooting week at Rhiwlas became an event of note, as did the grouse shoots on the surrounding mountains every August.

Traditional farming, as practiced by Richard Watkin Price, R. J. Lloyd Price's predecessor, took second place to the game farm, but it continued nevertheless under the management of the overseer John Williams. The expanding estate provided employment for gardeners, servants, carpenters, stone masons and roofers. A sawmill was established at Meloch, and a brush factory, the Rhiwlas Brush Works, whose logo was a woman wearing Welsh traditional costume and holding four brushes.

Lloyd Price also kept his own slaughterhouse and employed a local butcher. The meat was sold throughout Britain. Rhiwlas industries included a brickworks, which was established in 1891, and many local buildings, including Fron-goch Post Office (which still stands) and the gardeners' cottages, were built from this local product. A record of works also lists Lloyd Price as a 'Manufacturer and Grinder of aluminous non-polluting silicious earth to coarse and colour paper, cloth, artificial manure, polish, and metal soap makers, oil refining and disinfectant trades' [sic]. One product of this works, Fuller's Earth, was awarded the Second Prize Medal and Diploma at the Chicago Exhibition of 1893.

Lloyd Price's industries exploited a wealth of local natural resources. *The Liverpool Daily Post Courier* in December 1892 gave great prominence to discoveries made close to Fron-goch station. In addition to extensive beds of Fuller's Earth, there was an excellent deposit of rich blue clay from which aluminium could be extracted. This clay was suitable for the manufacture of the best dark red or chocolate brown bricks, terra-cotta ware and draining tiles, which the brickworks produced. The Fuller's Earth was also useful for manufacturers of Welsh woollens and for Liverpool wine refiners and refiners of other alcoholic drinks. The *Liverpool Daily Post Courier* correspondent prophesied that as the nucleus of several new industries Fron-goch was going to become a place of considerable importance.

Not content with these business interests, the squire also opened slate quarries at Caletwr near Llandderfel, but that venture was short-lived. He is also reputed to have set up a lime kiln at Garnedd. In an article on the 'Lost Industries of Rhiwlas' in the *Journal of the Meirioneth Historical and Record Society* 1962, J. H. Lloyd remembers farmers carting lime from the spot.

Another venture that received great publicity was 'Rhiwalis Table Waters'. This was water from Saint Beuno's Well at Mawnog Bach, which was on land belonging to the Red Lion at Bala. In an eight-page pamphlet, these wondrous waters were described as being 'colder than an ass's bray'. What gave the well's provenance greater credibility was the existence of an older Roman well beneath it.

The promotional pamphlet claimed that the water was good for the kidneys, the liver and the digestive organs. It could cure sore eyes and weak eyesight, and would ease feelings of repletion, flatulence or acidity. It could even cure animals. Indeed the pamphlet claimed that Captain Hopwood of Aberhirnant, who was huntsman of the Fourmart Hounds, would immerse his hounds in the well and so recharge their exhausted energies. The pamphlet was not alone with such claims: according to J. H. Lloyd, who himself had used the water to ease a sprained wrist, a Dr Williams, who practiced locally, believed strongly in the water's powers.

Lloyd Price visualised all his ventures connected: the Rhiwalis Waters, for example, would be coupled with the whisky venture, while casks for the whisky could be manufactured at the brush factory. He also had plans for manufacturing agricultural implements.

The location of Fron-goch was ideal for all these ventures: the Tryweryn river ensured a ready source of water and power, and the area was rich in woodland where alder, ash, birch, oak and sycamore grew in abundance. But another important factor in the development and potential success of these industrial experiments, including the whisky distillery, was the location of the railway station.

The Bala to Ffestiniog line was first mooted by Henry Robertson, Samuel Holland and others. The Great Western Railway and three local companies raised £156,000 of the required £190,000, and the line was opened on the 1st of November 1882. It operated for eighty years. The single track ran for twenty-two miles, climbing north along the Tryweryn Valley from its station at Bala, passing through Fron-goch Station and, following the river and bisecting the two Arenig mountains, ending at Blaenau Ffestiniog. At Arenig the line connected with the nearby granite quarries. The railway venture involved the building of forty-two bridges and sixteen viaducts. Its original purpose was to carry slates to the English Midlands but it also became an important passenger service, and provided five or six services daily up to the time of its closure. It was this line, with its connections to Holyhead, that made Fron-goch an ideal place for the internment of the Irish insurgents.

Nearly thirty years earlier, this railway line was also central to all Lloyd Price's ambitious schemes, including that most ambitious venture, the whisky distillery, which was to become home to the Irish internees.

In 1889, after water samples were taken and it was determined that the highest standard was to be found at the nearby Tai'r Felin brook, the Welsh Whisky Distillery Co. Ltd. was registered with a capital of £100,000; this was divided into 19,960 shares at £5, and 200 shares at £1. A parcel of land measuring '5 acres, 3 roods and 19 perches' was earmarked for the new distillery. Permission was granted to extract water from Tai'r Felin brook and also water and gravel from the Tryweryn river. Permission was also granted for quarrying local stone to build the distillery, the workers' cottages and the boundary walls.

Advertising and public relations were Lloyd Price's forte and he published a pamphlet named *The Truth* whose title page carries the following verse, which was no doubt penned by Lloyd Price himself:

> *Hir oes i'r Frenhines,*
> *Hir oes yn ddi-lyth,*
> *Hir oes i'r iaith annwyl*
> *A Chymru am byth.*

In essence, the jingle wishes an unflagging long life to the Queen, to the Welsh language and to Wales.

Beneath the verse is an exhortation to 'Drink Welsh Whisky', followed by an illustration of a John Jones dancing and presenting a bottle of Welsh whisky to a Jenny Jones with the jingle:

> 'Why with capers so many
> John Jones, gay you are?'
> 'Welsh Whisky, dear Jenny
> From Bala 'bur ddah'.

'Bur ddah', which should read 'bur dda', means good, or pure and good.

The pamphlet also names the people behind the venture: the Chairman, F. Richmond of Messrs Young & Co. from the Seel Street Distillery, Liverpool; director A. W. Ridley from the Mile End Distillery, London; H. Woodward of Seel Street, and F. Roberts of Phillips & Co, Bristol. All the officials, save for Lloyd Price himself, were prominent in the whisky trade.

On the 26th of December 1892 the *Liverpool Daily Courier* carried the following description of the distillery:

A noble building close to the Railway Station, and obvious therefore, as the saying goes, to the meanest observer, although as yet, the Directors of the Company have not considered it necessary to advertise its existence to the passing Railway Traveller by painting any name or description upon its massive walls, erected as they are from the handsome and durable grey granite of the country.

The company had grand plans. Between 1889 and 1890 several different names were registered for future brands; these included 'Black Prince', 'Men of Harlech', 'Maid of Llangollen', 'Saint David', 'Taffy', 'Welsh Rare Bit', 'Bells of Aberdovey' and 'The Leek'. The description of the whisky in *The Truth* reflects Lloyd Price the public relations man at his best. Although not officially credited to him, it is unlikely to have been penned by anyone else, the rhetoric reflecting the paeans of praise he wrote to various dogs and horses on his estate:

...the most wonderful whisky that ever drove the skeleton from the feast, or painted landscapes in the brain of man. It is the mingled souls of peat and barley, washed white within the rivers of the Tryweryn. In it you will find the sunshine and shadow that chased each other over the billowy fields, the breath of June, the carol of the lark, the dew of night, the wealth of summer, the autumn's rich content, all golden and imprisoned light. Drink it and you will hear the voice of men and maidens singing the 'Harvest Home' mingled with the laughter of children. Drink it, and you will feel within your blood the startled dawns, the dreamy tawny husks of perfect days. Drink it, and within your soul will burn the bardic fire of the Cymri, and their law-abiding earnestness. For many years this liquid joy has been within staves of oak, longing to touch the lips of man, nor will its prototype from the Sherry Casks disdain the more dulcet labial entanglement with any New or Old Woman.

The first amber drops of Welsh whisky passed through the copper tubes of the distillery in August 1889, and initially the bottles bore labels portraying Mrs Lloyd Price in fancy dress enthusiastically drinking the whisky. Earlier that year, Lloyd Price had engaged in poetic repartee with Sir Wilfred Lawson, the Member of Parliament for Cockermouth, who was a staunch teetotaler and was known as the Laureate of the Commons. Lawson had visited Bala on the 7th of June and had thundered against the demon drink, addressing his audience from the bridge that crosses the river Dee. Lloyd Price wrote to him:

> On Game of Temperance intent
> In accent clear and loud,
> Sir Wilfred on his usual bent
> Talks to the Bala crowd,
> From Bridge which Deva's wizard stream
> Spans nigh to Bala Lake;
> With honeyed words that flow like cream,
> He would the drunkard shake,
> He points out how that of the Dee
> Which neath his cork soles flows
> The products all that you and me
> Should trust beneath our nose.

Lawson must have replied, for on the 3rd of July Lloyd Price sent another poem to the MP:

> Your reply, my dear Wilfred, was welcome to me,
> And your muse, as of yore, reels off glibly and free,
> An advertisement bold your verses become,
> To strike Eno's Fruit Salt and Pears and Co. dumb –
> Now part of your grievance of poor little Wales,
> Of which your friend Ellis MP tells such tales,

Will soon be redressed, and none too soon too,
When she can proudly point to her own Mountain Dew.
And Ireland and Scotia will both cease to boast
When Welsh 'white eye' has got them both on toast,
And the still-born idea will not die still-born
When fame sounds Welsh Whiskey's praise loud on the horn.
In conclusion, I'm glad my dear Wilfred, to see
You're not quite so intolerant as you used to be,
Since you've come to praising up Hock and Dry Sillery
You may end up in the chair of the Wild Welsh Distillery,
The first stone of which, should you credit all tales
Will be laid by the Queen on her visit to Wales.

Lloyd Price's prediction that Queen Victoria would open the distillery was rather over-optimistic, but later that year, in September, when she visited the area and stayed at nearby Pale Hall, she was presented with a cask of Fron-goch whisky by Lloyd Price. Although the product never received the Royal Warrant, it was thereafter advertised as 'Royal Welsh Whisky'. It is said that during this visit, as she was presented with a picture of Bala Lake, Victoria delivered a speech in Welsh, the only occasion during her reign when she turned to 'the Language of Heaven'. The speech involved five words and did not make much sense. The cask of Welsh Whisky was duly delivered to Windsor Castle in 1891 where, as Lloyd Price commented at the time, it awaited 'the Royal consumption'.

Another cask was presented to the Prince of Wales in 1894 by the Bala Lodge of Freemasons (the Prince, traditionally, was the Grand Master of Britain's Lodges). The cask was made of light oak with golden hoops and bore a picture of Mrs Lloyd Price in Welsh dress – the same logo that appeared on the bottles. The present squire of Rhiwlas, Robin Price, knows that the cask remained untouched until as late as 1975.

An advertising poster for Welsh Whisky published in 1895,

which is held by the National Library of Wales, bears a copy of the certificate signed by the assessor, Granville R. Sharpe, certifying that the whisky possessed 'great purity of composition' and was 'thoroughly matured, and entirely free from all constituents of an injurious or undesirable character'. The certificate states that it was 'soft and pleasing to the palate' and was 'a perfectly sound and wholesome Whisky'.

Despite his pioneering enterprises, Lloyd Price was not universally admired. In his poem to Wilfred Lawson he mentions the grievances voiced by 'your friend, Ellis MP', which refers to Tom Ellis, the Liberal Member for Meirionnydd from 1886 to 1899. One of the founders of *Cymru Fydd* [Young Wales] whose main objective was to gain self-government for Wales, he was brought up at Cynlas on the Rhiwlas estate, and he was an outspoken critic of the local squire. Lloyd Price's great ambition had blinded him to the needs of his tenants and many other local people, and he antagonized them by his behaviour. Indeed he was often compared unfavourably to his predecessor, Richard Watkin Price, his grandfather. Richard Watkin was held in high regard despite the fact that, following the 1859 General Election, he had punished some of his tenants for voting against his great friend, the Tory Sir Watkin Williams Wynne. Of the twenty-one of his tenants who had not voted Tory, he evicted five and raised the rents of the rest. The strategy of threatening tenants unless they voted in accordance with his wishes was referred to as 'the Screw'. These tactics must have worked, as not one of the Rhiwlas tenants voted against the Tory candidate in 1865.

Yet despite this behaviour, Richard Watkin had been a progressive farmer who did much good. In contrast, his grandson's dream of turning Rhiwlas into a huge game estate antagonized the common people. As Einion Wyn Thomas observes, the establishment of a game farm was nothing new, but what made Lloyd Price different was the manner in which he did so: he laid down strict rules stating that no tenant should own more than two dogs; no tenant was allowed to shoot without the prior permission of the squire; no tenant could interfere in any way with the game, and indeed, in one area – Arenig Fach – no tenant was allowed to gather his sheep without the permission of one of the keepers. Even then, only the squire's shepherds and dogs could be used.

Lloyd Price transformed the Rhiwlas Estate with little regard for the effect this would have on his tenants. The proliferation of game created by the game farm naturally attracted poachers, but, as Einion Wyn Thomas notes, poaching in the area at that time was not committed in order to feed local families. Instead it became a political act. Indeed, it practically degenerated into a war between the estate and the common people. In the lead-up to the General Election in 1868, the Screw was at work again, and the tenants' reaction was to kill as many Rhiwlas pheasants as possible. According to a report in *Y Faner* at the time, the gang responsible was so powerful that no keeper would dare try to stop them, and just in case some of the Rhiwlas tenants were tempted to waver, the most militant among them warned that 'matches came cheap'. The Screw was now being applied by the tenants against the gentry. A few days before the Election, the Tory withdrew his nomination, and no Tory has since represented Meirionnydd.

Between 1867 and 1870 there were seventy cases of poaching brought before Bala magistrates, forty-nine of which involved Rhiwlas. The most famous case followed a battle between a dozen poachers and six Rhiwlas keepers at Tynffridd near Llanfor on the 19th of November 1867. There was an exchange of gunfire and physical blows. Three poachers were arrested, all of whom were sons of respectable local farmers: Edward Owen, aged twenty-one; Evan Jones, aged sixteen, and John Roberts, aged twenty-five. The three were mercilessly set upon by the keepers. Indeed, one of the three, John Roberts, brought an action against the keepers for attacking him on another occasion. He described his attackers as behaving like highwaymen, but in a hearing that was held behind closed doors, the keepers were found not guilty. This provoked letters of complaint to the local paper, *Y Faner* [The Flag], condemning the bench. One correspondent wrote: 'Before the common people can respect the law, firstly they must be convinced that the gentry operate fairly.'

At the hearing for the three poachers, the court was teeming with supporters. Such was the bad feeling that the magistrates later released them on surety, on condition of good behaviour. Had they been dealt with severely, it could have led to open war. It has been suggested that Lloyd Price had been leant on to influence his keepers to keep a lower profile. He certainly learnt from the experience, for he later admitted that the Tynffridd incident had been caused less by poaching matters and more by personal hatred towards himself.

In an article in *Y Seren* [The Star] following the squire's death in 1923, an 'Occasional Correspondent', looking back at this period, describes the events as having had nothing in common with ordinary poaching:

> This was not a mere hunt by a poor labourer for the occasional hare or pheasant that would put in his pocket a shilling or half-a-crown now and then. This was a battle by responsible farmers' sons and the most respectable young men in the district. This was a protest against a rabble of unprincipled and devious English gamekeepers brought to our land to violate the inhabitants, to bring false accusations against them and to make their lives pitiful for years.

What happened at Tynffridd, he claims, was a war. This war arose out of conditions that were not dissimilar to conditions in

Ireland. In Ireland at the time, Michael Davitt and the Land League were slowly but surely winning the Land War against unscrupulous landlords, and it was in this connection that Davitt addressed a meeting at nearby Blaenau Ffestiniog in the spring of 1885 (a meeting that was attended by Lloyd George). Davitt's part in the struggle was known to Tom Ellis, and it was the success of the Land League that led to the establishment of the Land Commission in 1893, in which Ellis was a critical witness.

The tenants' complaints were heard at the Land Commission hearing held at Bala. John Jones of Ty'n Celyn complained that pheasants had been introduced to every copse on his land, and that the birds caused great damage to his crops. Dafydd Roberts of Llannerch Eryr could not produce enough fodder to keep four cows, four calves and two horses because of the proliferation of rabbits on his land. It was claimed that on the 11th of October 1883 eight hunters managed to shoot over a thousand rabbits on just one small area of the farmland. The farm was described as constituting a single huge warren.

The evidence that Tom Ellis produced at the Land Commission hearing is quoted extensively in the biography that his son T. I. Ellis wrote. At the hearing, Ellis praised the predecessor of R. J. Lloyd Price as a man of note, a true leader in the agricultural industry, and as someone who was on neighbourly terms with the farmers and farms of his estate. During his tenure as squire there had only been one keeper on the estate and very little game, but under his successor, who had come into possession of the estate in 1864, things had changed. This was when the grand era of hunting and shooting at Rhiwlas had begun. Ellis declared:

A crowd of English and Scotch gamekeepers was introduced and dotted all over the estate. I cannot describe the repugnance to and loathing for the game preserving system engendered by the overbearing conduct and petty tyranny of these gamekeepers, by the monstrous increase of rabbits and pheasants, and by the depredations of game on the crops of struggling farmers.

The transformation is reflected in the change recorded between the Census of 1861 and that of 1871: during that decade the number of gamekeepers rose from one, who was a Welshman, to fourteen – ten of whom were English and two of whom were Scottish. As part of his testimony, Tom Ellis spoke of an incident which had affected him deeply when he was a child of eight. In February 1867, while his father was away, one of his dogs had chased a hare but had not been able to catch it. That night a keeper, George Stretton, called to complain. The following morning, Tom Ellis' father was summoned to Rhiwlas with his two dogs. The dogs were shot.

Ellis' father was advised by the sole Welsh keeper that he should do something about the incident if he wanted to avoid being evicted, but on the 27th of September he was summoned to leave his holding. Following weeks of negotiations he was permitted to stay, but with an increase in rent of £10 per annum. He had no choice but to accept. Tom Ellis remarked to the Land Commission hearing: 'My father has forgiven, and wishes to forget it all. But these things cannot be forgotten...'

Indeed Tom Ellis did not forget. In June 1891 he was present at a party that was held to celebrate the coming of age of R. J. Lloyd Price's heir. The Rhiwlas tenants had been invited, as had the gentry. Here again Ellis pulled no punches. As *Y Seren* reported on the 6th of June, he expressed regret that the heir, though he had a Welsh name, could not speak his nation's tongue:

Honour will come to him should he become a soldier fighting against ignorance, poverty and misery. In this beautiful part of Wales, where his estate lies, namely the Tryweryn area, one out of every twenty is a pauper. It will be within his power as a landowner as a magistrate, and as a warden to help remove this mark of shame on the community.

There are taverns in towns and villages on the estate, yet not one public library. He is heir to an estate of smallholders. It is cheerful for him, and for us to see their hopeful faces today, but I know that the lines on their faces are an expression of the concern, the trials and the hard life that falls so heavily on their lot: and should he remember all this in all his dealings with them, then blessed may he be. It is a matter of regret that there is neither here on this estate nor in other parts of Wales an agricultural school such as those in Denmark...

He is also heir to an area of Welsh land - and it is hoped that he realizes that Wales is the land of awakening – that a renewed national life pervades it; that there is a new ideal amongst us regarding dignity, work and labour, and a new growth of self-confidence as a nation.

This was a defiant address – indeed, under such circumstances, a brave address for the MP to make. It is interesting to note that on the same occasion Michael D. Jones praised R. J. Lloyd Price and Richard Watkin Price, the predecessors of the heir to the estate. The former he praised for building roads and promoting better agricultural efficiency among his tenants, and the latter for establishing the brush factory and engaging in drainage work on the estate. He made no mention of the whisky enterprise.

It is curious that two prominent Welshmen, one an MP and the other a minister of religion, a staunch nationalist and the prime mover behind the Welsh colonisation of Patagonia, should have held such different views. Indeed, Michael D. Jones, whose own mother had been evicted for not conforming to her landlord's political views, had been instrumental in inviting

Michael Davitt to Blaenau Ffestiniog in 1885. The answer to this curious inconsistency may lie in the fact that both Lloyd Price and Michael D. Jones were Freemasons.

The heir to Rhiwlas, Robert Kendrick Price, did not fulfil many of the hopes expressed by Tom Ellis, but one of Ellis' hopes was realized: the Welsh Whisky Company went to the wall, after a mere ten years in operation. Some have fancifully blamed the Welsh temperance movement for the company's demise. There are many stories about farmers who were only willing to bring in grain after dark, and stories that the whisky was only moved at night in order to avoid local religious friction. This may have played its part in the staunchly nonconformist locality, but if feelings were so high, this does not account for the fact that some thirty local people worked at the distillery and that the workforce, including those involved in the bottling at the White Lion at Bala, numbered around a hundred. Local tradition has even blamed the religious revival of 1904–1905 for the distillery's demise, but the business had folded five years previously.

A more plausible explanation is that the whisky was of inferior quality. An article by H. A. Lloyd in the *Country Quest* of October 1966 states that the whisky, while fine in casks, matured backwards in bottles. This suggestion is repeated in an article in *Harper's Manual:*

> The whisky was not maturing properly; it remained rawish, crude and practically flavourless for a pure malt product and a market could not be found for it on its supposed merits at a profitable price.

The whisky, the article continues, lay in the distillery warehouses 'eating its head off' for want of customers.

It would appear that many of the casks from the accumulating stock were sold off at a loss. Ultimately the whole of the remaining stock came under the auctioneer's hammer in London where it sold for less than half – even as low as one third – of the cost of production, the expense of storage and interest paid against expenses.

Following two board meetings on the 16th of December 1898 and the 3rd of January 1899, the company was wound up, and on the 24th of April 1900, the distillery site was bought by William Owen, owner of the White Lion, Bala for £5,000. He also bought off the remaining leasehold for £250. Rhiwlas ran into difficulties later: in *Cofio Tryweryn* [Remembering Tryweryn], Watcyn Ll. Jones claims that in 1905, 1911 and 1917 it was heavily mortgaged, which left the estate deeply in debt.

The whisky business must have been sorely missed by the trout that teemed in the Tryweryn river – it would appear that they had thrived on the mash of barley and hot water that was regularly emptied into the stream.

Very little of the Fron-goch whisky has survived. One bottle is held by the National Museum of Wales. It is said that another exists at Llandyrnog and three in an area of Pembrokeshire. A Bala resident owned as many as seven bottles until 1969. He then presented Prince Charles with six of the bottles to mark his investiture as Prince of Wales, while the seventh was presented to Rhiwlas. The last bottle to go on open sale made £1,350 at an auction held in September 2001.

The distillery fell into disuse until it was appropriated by the Government and adapted as a holding camp for captured German prisoners in 1914. Some local people believe that German prisoners returned in 1917, but this is debatable. It remained largely unused until the site was gradually cleared during the 1930s. Some of the stones from the distillery were used to build two houses at Llanuwchllyn, and – somewhat ironically – it seems that Talybont Chapel near Fron-goch was restored with stone that had once housed one of the sources of the demon drink.

R. J. Lloyd Price died on January 9th, 1923, some forty-six years after he built his own mausoleum with money made from a bet he placed on a horse named Bendigo in the Jubilee Stakes of 1887. Price was eighty years old. Above the vault door are carved the words:

As to my latter end I go, to meet my Jubilee,
I thank my good horse Bendigo, who built this tomb for me.

Despite the troubles caused by his gamekeepers, R. J. Lloyd Price is remembered more as a pioneering eccentric than as a tyrannical landlord. Meanwhile, at the time of his death, many of those who had been interned in his old distillery in 1916 were still busily killing each other in the seemingly endless Irish Civil War. The evening before he died, five Republicans were executed by the Free State Government for treachery, and in the days between his death and his funeral, another nineteen were executed for illegal possession of arms. The seeds sown at Fron-goch had sprouted and ripened into a bloody harvest.

3
Frogmore

The inhabitants of the Bala area learned of developments at Fron-goch through their local paper, *Y Seren*. On the 10th of June – the day after the arrival of the first batch of prisoners – readers were informed that around two hundred guards had arrived, while on the 24th of June the paper reported that some six hundred rebels had arrived. The prisoners were known as 'the Sinn Féiners', the paper explained, and hundreds were arriving daily. It also revealed that the camp doctor was a Mr Peters and that visitors to the prisoners had already been allowed in. Visiting days, announced the paper, were Tuesdays and Thursdays.

When the first three prisoners arrived – appropriately numbered 1, 2 and 3 – they must have felt rather at a loss as city men in the country. These three, James Coughlan, Thomas Boylan and Herbert Conroy, were Dubliners. As the train pulled in at the station, their first view would have been of a grey, forbidding-looking building dominated by a tall brick chimney and overlooking a small hamlet surrounded by open country.

Their long journey – and that of the others who followed – had begun at Richmond Barracks or Kilmainham Jail, from where they had been marched to North Wall. Here they were herded aboard the cattle ship the *Slieve Bloom* and ferried to Holyhead and on to various English and Scottish prisons, before being transferred later to Fron-goch.

Most of the men were roughly treated as they were escorted through the streets and while they were on board the cattle boat. In an interview for a Welsh television documentary made by *Ffilmiau'r Nant* in 1988, Ambrose Byrne, a Dubliner, recalled the scorn of his fellow citizens towards him and his comrades: they threw cups and saucers at them as they marched along Sackville Street and Thomas Street to Inchicore Barracks.

Joe Clarke, who at his funeral in 1976 was described by Éamon Mac Thomáis as the greatest of the Fenians, recalled in a personal interview how he had been prodded along at the point of a bayonet:

> We were mocked mercilessly by some of our fellow Irish among the thousands that had flocked to the streets to see 'those Sinn Féin fools'. Rotten apples and even worse things were thrown at us. Naturally, we felt low. Others in the crowd, however, waved green banners and sang the old rebel songs. We marched to the boat with our heads, if not our hearts, held high.

On the boat, a fortunate few were allowed to sail as third-class passengers, but the majority were kept below decks in the cattle pens. Indeed, on some voyages, the men had to share the pens with the cattle.

Brian O'Higgins described an experience that many of his comrades must have shared. As the rebels approached the boat, a number of British soldiers were about to embark. The soldiers were halted by an order from an officer: 'Stay where you are, men. Let the dirt go first.'

The filthy, smelly conditions were bad enough, but there was also the continual threat of German torpedoes. All the lifebelts were taken by the soldiers. Michael Brennan of Clare was herded on to the boat among the cattle, and experienced the horror of the boat turning and twisting as it tried to avoid torpedoes, which drove the unfortunate cattle wild with fright.

Before the voyage the men were handed a single dog biscuit each, but were given nothing to drink, not even water. M. J. O'Connor and his party, however, were more fortunate than most. They sailed on the 6th of June on what he described as 'the ocean greyhound'. They were placed in a fairly comfortable but badly ventilated compartment meant for third-class passengers. O'Connor, who had been arrested at Tralee, recalled his experiences in his book *Stone Walls:*

> The time was whiled away chatting, smoking and singing. It was interesting, if not amusing, to see the soldiers and their officers listening intently to the singing of 'The Felons of Our Land' as the ship touched the Welsh shore about 12.45, English time. With the exception of a young Enniscorthy chap, all the party escaped sea-sickness.

Another who shared a similar experience was Joe O'Doherty from Derry, whose reminiscences about the voyage were recorded on tape. As he and his companions were herded towards the boat, they were pelted with stones by an angry mob. The boat had not been cleaned and cow dung covered the bottom of the hold. The only light to enter the locked hold was what came through one of the half-open hatches. Through that opening came a shaft of sunlight. One of the rebels rose, stood in that light and sang 'When Will the Day Break in Erin?' This incident left a lasting impression on O'Doherty.

M. J. O'Connor remembered the soldiers who were sent to meet them at the dockside in Holyhead. To the hilarity of the prisoners' escort, who were members of the Dublin Fusiliers, the soldiers who escorted the prisoners onto the train for Knutsford Jail were members of the Bantam Battalion, a battalion reserved for unusually short men. The prisoners sarcastically dubbed them the Grenadier Guards.

Within days of being sent to English prisons, the first batch of rebels was sent on to Fron-goch, located three miles west of Bala. The men, under armed escort, reached the camp by train. From the various prisons they would have been brought first to Crewe and then on through Chester before crossing the Welsh border near Wrexham. The train would have journeyed on through Rhiwabon, Llangollen and Bala Junction, and here it would have been diverted onto the Ffestiniog line. Fron-goch Station stood less than twenty yards from the camp's two compounds.

Many of the men later testified to the feeling of joy as they crossed the Welsh border. M. J. O'Connor realised that the train had crossed into 'Gallant Little Wales' when he saw Great Western Railway signs alongside the line in both English and Welsh. He expressed regret that the Irish Railway Company did not follow the same example by using the Irish language on its signs and notices.

A letter that I received from W. J. Brennan-Whitmore repeats almost verbatim the account of his first impressions which appeared in his memoir *With the Irish in Frongoch*. Written on the 6th of June 1971 the letter refers to my earlier letter to him as 'a refreshing breeze straight from your dear Welsh hills. We all have fond memories of your landscape and people.' He went on to quote one of his comrades who described the Welsh with affection:

> We found all the Welsh people we came into contact with cheery. I heard another remark as we pulled out of a wayside station: 'They're so different to the English, who look at you in the way a cow looks over a hedge. And I'm not flattering.'

Brennan-Whitemore and M. J. O'Connor both describe the experience of arriving at Fron-goch. O'Connor had prepared himself for a three-mile march to the camp, probably thinking that the line ended at Bala. He was pleasantly surprised to find that the camp was so close to the station. However, he could not understand how such a place could be described as a camp:

> It would take a pen far more facile and descriptive than mine to give even a fair description of the Camp. Why it

was dubbed a camp, I can never understand. Fancy to yourself a long, dismal-looking three storeyed stone building which was up to the outbreak of war a malt store used in connection with the adjoining distillery – also disused. The windows were few, small and of the most primitive kind, those on the ground floor and at the end of the building being barred. This, surely, was not an inviting place in which to be interned indefinitely. The weather, which in the morning was fine, had turned cold and showery and did not help to make our new surroundings look any way pleasant. We were consoled, however, by the appearance at the windows of some fellow-prisoners who, when signalling to greet us, were ordered to 'keep in from those windows'.

On seeing the camp for the first time, Brennan-Whitmore felt similarly disheartened. He described an impression of dreariness and inhospitality. When he arrived, the yard was deserted but the windows in the background were filled with faces, all shouting their greetings, which the new arrivals tried to answer as enthusiastically as possible.

In his account *B'fhiú an Braon Fola* [Worth a Drop of Blood] Séamas Ó Maoileoin describes his surprise when he first saw the Meirionnydd countryside through the carriage window towards the end of his hundred and twenty mile journey from Wakefield Jail. At first glance, he thought, the landscape was similar to that of Connemara:

But I am certain that there is nowhere in Connemara as remote, as lonely, as cold and as dreary. There were very few houses in the neighbourhood, and despite the fact that the town of Bala, standing beside a lake of the same name, was only three miles away and had a population of over a thousand, we scarcely saw a man or a stranger passing by.

Billy Mullins of Tralee could remember every minute of his

journey from Wormood Scrubs. In an interview on Welsh television he said that he did not know where he was headed, and did not care a damn anyway:

> We were prisoners, and they could do anything they wished with us ….We had been imprisoned without trial. We knew not when we would be released…

Michael Collins was kinder about the appearance of the area. Writing from Hut 7 in the Upper Camp (North Camp) to his sister Hannie, he described his journey 'thro a most engaging country'. In his biography of Collins, Rex Taylor attempts to describe the Fron-goch landscape in neutral terms, and he too compares it to Ireland:

> The area in which the camp was situated was rough moorland country, agreeable country, but void of any particular distinction; a countryside suitable, because of its wildness, for the sports of shooting and fishing. To many of the internees, however, it recalled the situation of their homes in Ireland, with its background of mountains, and rich, full growths of heather, scattered trees and ferns.

There was something else that reminded them of home. The visiting camp workers and tradesmen all spoke Welsh. This provoked in many of the men a sense of guilt for losing much of their native tongue, and imbued them with a determination to regain what they had lost. This is emphasised by numerous historians and biographers. For example, Rex Taylor observes of Collins:

> He interested himself keenly in the Welsh tradesmen who came to do jobs in the camp and who spoke their native language with the pride of the undefeated. Hearing them speak, seeing them at their work, determined him yet again to seek out the true value of his native tongue. It was

something for which other Irish patriots had worked for in the past: the idea of a native language as a means of stimulation towards freedom. And even now, at Frongoch and in other places of internment and imprisonment, the idea of a native language was being rapidly fostered. It was in such places that the tremendous surge of nationalism was really begun, which was, later, to sweep to victory over the British, politically and otherwise.

Margery Forester makes the same point in *Michael Collins: The Lost Leader*:

> Beyond the camp to the south flowed the river Tryweryn. Rising away to the north in the wild beauty of the Welsh countryside moorland peaks with names like Carnedd-y-Filast and Cader Benllyn reminded the Irish exiles that here lived a people whose country and language were in many ways as remote from England as Ireland itself.

Batt O'Connor, one of the internees who later became close friends with Collins, reveals in *With Michael Collins in the Fight for Irish Independence*:

> One thing at Frongoch greatly impressed us. All the workmen who came to carry out any plumbing or repairs at the camp spoke the Welsh language. This was a great surprise for most of us. We marvelled at the fine national spirit of those men, and their love for their native tongue, that they should have been able to preserve it, and they living alongside the English without even a bay between. It gave us a feeling of wholesome humility beside those Welsh fellows to hear them chatting away to each other without a word of English, while we were laboriously re-learning the language of our fathers.

Some of the men, especially those from the West, were fluent Irish speakers and as the camp got organised, Irish and Welsh classes were included in the curriculum.

The maximum number of men who were held at Fron-goch was nine hundred and sixty three in South Camp and eight hundred and ninety six in North Camp. In *Frongoch: University of Freedom* Sean O Mahony lists 1,804 names of men who were interned at the Meirionnydd camp. He expresses regret that the list is incomplete and that the Home Office seemed not to have an extant record of the men – indeed O Mahony's list is by far the most complete record available. Of these, he lists nine hundred and twenty six from Dublin City and County, three hundred and twenty two from County Galway, a hundred and fifty from County Wexford, and ninety two from County Cork. In all, thirty two Irish counties were represented. Five men are listed as being resident in England although many more had lived there, but it is impossible to know how many, like Jim Mooney, had lived in Wales.

O Mahony elaborates on the biographical details of some of the internees. Jeremiah Reardon, one of the oldest in the camp, had been jailed in 1881 for his part in the Land League activities. James Stritch had been involved in an even earlier episode – the incident in 1867 in Manchester that became known as 'The Smashing of the Van', when two Fenians, Thomas Kelly and Timothy Deasy, were freed from a horse-drawn prison van. During the skirmish, a member of the Manchester Constabulary, Sergeant Charles Brett, was killed. As a result, three rebels involved – William Allen, Michael Larkin and Michael O'Brien – were all executed.

Others had colourful histories of a different sort: Barney O'Driscoll was an ex-officer in the American National Guard. Frank Bulfin from County Offaly had a brother who owned one of Argentina's largest farms. He had a brother, William, at Fron-goch and his nephew Eamon had been at the General Post Office on the Easter Monday, where he had raised the

Tricolour flag. Dan O'Mahony from County Kerry had been a big game hunter in South Africa, where he refused to join a British coup aimed at toppling the Boer government. Mort O'Connor, also from Kerry, had been a gold prospector in the Klondike.

However, as O Mahony stresses, the great majority of the internees were ordinary workers, a point also made by W. J. Brennan-Whitmore. They were a mixture of painters and decorators, clerks, tailors, van drivers, porters, printers, carters and labourers.

Most of the men were young; indeed about eighty of them were eighteen years old or younger. In his memoir, *Enchanted by Dreams*, Joe Good estimates that some forty per cent of the internees were married men.

Many of the prisoners were members of the same family. O Mahony lists the Ring brothers, five of whom had taken part in the Rising. There were Charles, James and John Goulding; Seán T. and Michael O'Kelly; Ambrose and Laurence Byrne and Bob and Daniel Holland. The Hollands belonged to a staunch rebel family. Their home in Inchicore had held seven cases of American rifles during the weeks preceding the Rising. In his witness statement to the Bureau of Military History in 1949, Bob Holland reported:

> A spurt was put on to encourage the men to get their hands on service rifles and .305 ammunition. These could be bought from British soldiers who were returning from leave from France and other war zones. Prices ranged from £5 to £7 per rifle, and if a soldier was drunk enough we relieved him of his rifle without compensation.

Other sets of brothers included John and Joseph Guilfoyle, and John, Joseph and Thomas Kearns, all from Dublin. Other families from Dublin included Patrick and Donald Ward; Tommy and John O'Connor; the Tully brothers; John and Pat

Poole; James, Charles and Joseph Tallon (O'Tallamhain), and John and William O'Carroll, whose father, Peter, was later shot and killed by the Black and Tans because he was mistaken for one of his sons. And the list goes on.

The strength of family ties among the rebels is evident in the fact that in his incomplete list of nine hundred and twenty six internees from Dublin City and County alone, O Mahony refers to almost fifty sets of two or more brothers who shared an address. It is obvious that there were many more brothers living at different addresses. O Mahony also notes two instances of fathers and sons being together at Fron-goch: Patrick and Joseph Fleming from Galway, who joined Liam Mellows in the Rising, and Henry and Séamus Dobbyn from Belfast.

The O'Reilly family was another case of father and sons being interned together. The O'Reillys were among those who had met at Hugh Holohan's home in 77 Amiens Street to plan the Rising. Holohan was sent to Fron-goch, as were six members of the O'Reilly family who took part in the Rising: the father, John Kevin, who was later to write 'Wrap the Green Flag Round Me, Boys', and five of his sons. John Kevin and at least three of his sons, Desmond, Kevin and Sam, were imprisoned in Fron-goch. Sam was one of a group sent to London by Cathal Brugha on the occasion of the reopening of Parliament on the 15th of October 1918; their task was to shoot the Minister responsible for announcing the onset of conscription in Ireland. The group waited, ready, in the House of Commons gallery, but luckily for the Minister in question, the announcement was not made and the would-be assassins returned to Dublin. During the War of Independence, Sam went on hunger strike in Mountjoy Jail, and later on left for America. During the Civil War, the father and two of his sons took the Free State side while two sons were among the Republicans on the other side.

Among those at Fron-goch were a number of students from

Pearse's St Enda's College. These included Frank Burke and Joseph O'Connor, who was known as Little Joe, both from Dublin; Eamon Bulfin and Joseph Sweeney from Donegal; J. Kilgallon from America; Fintan Murphy from London; Brian Joyce from Galway, and Desmond Ryan from Dublin. There were also two gardeners from St Enda's: Michael MacRuarí and Paddy Donnelly.

As well as those who had seen action during Easter Week there were many internees who had been arrested and held for no apparent reason. Their only mistake was to have been in the wrong place at the wrong time. Rex Taylor observes that this was the factor that caused ambiguity in the use of the words 'internees' and 'prisoners': without having been charged, the men could not be regarded as prisoners of war. In a letter to Seán Deasy on the 12th of September Collins wrote that in his estimation, at least a quarter of the men in North Camp were completely ignorant of the Rising. One man he knew, a labourer, had told him that he was forced off the street during the search for rebel soldiers. His only crime appeared to be that he was walking the streets.

Before being moved to Fron-goch, every internee was issued with an Internment Form. Beneath each man's name appeared the following declaration:

> Notice is hereby given to the above name that an Order has been made by the Secretary of State under Regulation 14B of the Defence of the Realm Regulations directing that he shall be interned at the place of Internment at Frongoch.
>
> The Order is made on the grounds that he is of hostile association and a member of an organisation called the Irish Volunteers or an organisation called the Citizen Army, which have promoted armed insurrection against His Majesty and is reasonably suspected of having favoured, promoted or assisted in armed insurrection against His majesty.

47. Some of the Camp's chief officers and families outside the Commandant's home: Captain Sholto Douglas; Lt Grimston – known as Brimstone; Lt Burns; Armstrong, one of the Censors; Miss Lambert; Lt J. D. Watson; Lt C. Lambert; Lt Col Heygate-Lambert; Mrs Heygate-Lambert; Capt Powys Keeke, Captain of the Guards, and Lt Bevan, another Censor.

48. A general view of South Camp taken by a local photographer. Note the description.

49. A drawing of one of the huts in the North Camp.

> 'I've run the outlaws brief careers *7/4*
> And borne his load of ill
> His troubled rest & waking fear
> With fixed sustaining will .
> And should his last dread chance befall
> E'er that would welcome be
> In death I'd love thee more than all
> Aeudla geal mo croidhe .
>
>   Miceál Ua Coilleasn
>   Capt   IR A.
>   Clonakilty
>   Cork.
>   Frongoch 1916.

Autograph entry written in Frongoch by Michael Collins.

50. Michael Collins' handwriting and autograph in one of the books kept by a Fron-goch internee.

51. The men organising their own activities
in one of the huts.

Prisoners of War.

No
Stamp
Required

*Copy of P.O.W. status envelope. Letter written by Jack MacDonagh, brother
of executed 1916 leader, Thomas, to his sister, a Dublin-based nun.*

OPENED BY
CENSOR.
1330

52. An official envelope issued by the
Censor for sending or
receiving letters.

53. The North camp's kitchen on the
field facing South Camp.

54. Michael Collins
in his early twenties.

55. Richard Mulcahy, Commander
in Chief of the Army in 1922.

56. Tomás MacCurtain,
Lord Mayor of Cork murdered by the
RIC 1920.

57. Terence MacSwiney,
Lord Mayor of Cork, who died in
Brixton Prison in 1920 after 74 days
on hunger strike.

58. MacSwiney's coffin being carried out of Cork Cathedral on the 30th of September 1920.

59. Members of Collins' Twelve Apostles: Joe Leonard, Jim Slattery, Joe Dolan, Gearóid O'Sullivan, Bill Stapleton and Charlie Dalton. Four of these, Slattery, Dalton, O'Sullivan and Stapleton, were at Fron-goch.

60. The Black Hand Gang. Were they jokers or members of a secret organisation?

61. & 62. A replica of the armoured car and Crossley troop truck that were used by Michael Collins on his last journey.

63. *The preliminary work for the toppling of the chimney stack. A Mr Larkin from London (left) was the demolition expert while one of the site's owners, Arthur Morris, Plas Deon, Llanuwchllyn stands between two of the workers on the right.*

64. *The distillery's chimney stack being demolished on the 13th of May, 1934.*

65. *The present incumbent of the Rhiwlas estate, Robin Price, with a rare bottle of Welsh whisky.*

66. The gate at Kilmainham Gaol opened with the aid of two Welsh Guards thus allowing the escape of Ernie O'Malley, Frank Teeling and Simon Donnelly in 1921.

67. Paddy Moran (left) and Thomas Whelan flanking one of the Kilmainham Gaol guards. They were among six hanged on the same day. Both of them as well as another of the six prisoners had been at Fron-goch.

68. Martin Savage, once at Fron-goch and one of the Twelve Apostles, killed in the Ashtown Road ambush on the 19th of December, 1919. Two other Fron-goch men, Seamus Robinson and Paddy Daly were involved.

70. Fron-goch Station is now just
another house in the village.

69. Fron-goch's shoemaker, Tom
Traynor, a father of ten who was executed on 26 April 1921.

71. This house was home to the Fron-goch Station Master;
it was later a Post Office.

72. These houses were built as homes for the distillery chiefs before they housed British Officers.

73. The old signal box at Fron-goch Station now stands in a back garden.

74. The school, Ysgol Bro Tryweryn, which stands on the site of the old distillery and South Camp.

75. The tri-lingual plaque by the roadside opposite the site where North Camp stood.

91

76. & 77. Two views of the hut which stands on the North Camp site, home of the local branch of the Women's Institute. It is unlikely to be a survivor of 1916.

Frongoch Camp,

adjoining Frengoch Railway Station
and Siding (G W.R) near BALA.

Unreserved Sale of

40 Excellent Sectional Barrack Huts.

78. An advert in a local paper offering forty of the Fron-goch huts for sale.

Several Corrugated Buildings and Sheds,
Quantity of Loose Timber, Corrugated
Sheets, Barb Wire &c., &c.

79. The shop at Fron-goch today, housing a small gallery of the old camp.

80. Many farmers bought the old Fron-goch barrack huts. This one survives as a garden shed in a village near Bala.

82. These two houses at Llanuwchllyn were built with reclaimed timber and bricks from the Fron-goch whisky distillery when it was demolished.

81. The inside of the hut shows the original timber panelling.

83. Capel Celyn village near Fron-goch, demolished and drowned by Liverpool Corporation in 1965.

84. Llyn Celyn, the reservoir dam completed. Its construction attracted Irishmen back to Fron-goch.

85. & 86. Defiant graffiti painted on a boulder when the remains of the village re-emerged during a severe drought.

87. The Capel Celyn memorial chapel. Some of the old gravestones were spared and moved to this site above the reservoir.

88. The National Museum in Dublin.

89. The Memorial Gardens in Dublin.

90. Wales still remembers Tryweryn.

The prisoners were given seven days to make a plea against this Order. Batt O'Connor named Henry Dixon as having been the only one to refuse initially to sign the declaration.

South Camp was the destination of the first nine hundred or so prisoners to arrive. North Camp, facing the old distillery building, was still in the process of being built as South Camp filled. With the exception of a few sick men, the previous occupants, the German prisoners, had been moved to other camps. One of those who remained was dying of tuberculosis. Séamas Ó Maoileoin could remember seeing two or three sick Germans in the camp hospital. These prisoners were considerably cheered when they heard the news that Kitchener had been drowned when his ship sank. Their joy would perhaps have been doubled had they realised that Kitchener was the man who had established, in South Africa, the first-ever internment camp.

There appears to have been a good relationship between the Irish prisoners and the remaining Germans. Joe Clarke vividly remembered the German language signs that were left on the walls. One notice that survived was *Trinke Wasser* [Drinking Water] inscribed above one of the taps. The internees, however, were refused permission to have notices in their own native language.

Seven Germans who died at Fron-goch were buried in the local churchyard along the main road from the camp. They are officially listed as W. Forster, H. Langenberg, A. Schirmer, P. H. Schroter, A. Stauch, P. Velleur and R. T. Waschkowitz. In March 1963 the bodies were disinterred and reburied in the German War Cemetery at Cannock Chase in Staffordshire. This was part of a general policy that involved reburying the bodies of five and a half thousand German soldiers who had died in Britain.

One piece of information that the Irish gleaned from the few remaining Germans was the fact that South Camp was preferable to North Camp. While the former was uncomfortable and oppressively hot in summer, the latter was extremely cold during the winter. The Germans lost more prisoners to the cold than they did to the stifling heat. Irish prisoners named the two camps Purgatory and Siberia.

In a letter to his sister Johanna on the 25th of August 1916, Michael Collins complained about the heat after he had been moved to South Camp:

> When one wakes the oppressive atmosphere is really quite terrible. In some unfavoured spots breathing is almost difficult in the mornings. Luckily I myself am at a window so don't suffer as much in this respect as others but then the other night which was wild & wet my bedclothes got very damp indeed.

South Camp consisted of a collection of buildings in a fenced-in square. The three-story storehouse that housed the dormitories stood on the west side, the main entrance was to the north, between the hospital and the censor's office on one side and the generator house on the other, while the drying room, where there was a furnace, stood nearby. To the east stood the distillery and the vat house, which had been turned into a coal bunker and workshops. The kitchen lay at the lower end of the vat house. To one side lay the refectory, which could seat fifteen hundred men. It could also be utilised as a hall and a place of worship. Within the square there were also huts that offered more sleeping space, and a dry canteen, a shop, a barber's shop and workshops for shoe repairing and tailoring.

On the outer limit of the north side stood sick rooms, and on the corner was a YMCA hut used for indoor activities – this was the meeting place for the internees' General Council. Further along was a garden and a wooden hut.

Around the outer boundary stretched a tangle of barbed wire and wooden platforms manned by armed sentries.

Between the barbed wire and the main road through the village stood a larger detached house and the officers' dwellings, two blocks of which still stand, their back windows looking down on the old distillery complex. Between South Camp and the Tryweryn river lay a three-acre vegetable garden and beyond that, a playing field.

Within the outer barbed wire fence ran a single strand of barbed wire stretched twelve feet above ground level. This was 'the fence of death': internees were allowed to hang their clothes on the lower strands that stretched beneath it but were not allowed to lean on it. They were warned that anyone foolish enough to try and escape would be shot. As Ambrose Byrne remarked: 'We were allowed to do anything but escape.'

Séamas Ó Maoileoin described his new home as a five-roomed building: three were large rooms that contained beds for between two and three hundred men, and the other two contained a hundred beds each. He described his first night as dark, dismal and sad. There was little room between the beds, the windows were few, and very little air could circulate. He observed that this would have been fine in its distillery days when the same rooms were used to dry grain, but using them as dormitories was another matter, especially during the summer heat.

M. J. O'Connor served time in both North and South camps, and in his book *Stone Walls* he describes both compounds. Registered as Prisoner No. 940, he was placed in Room 6 in South Camp. Here two beds had been made from wooden laths that rested on wooden trestles some two feet off the floor. A plain mattress of sorts, which was filled with straw, and a small straw pillow lay on the laths. These were in turn covered by three rough, dark-coloured blankets. He remarked that the mattress was so round in shape and so tightly packed with straw that sleeping on such a bed was like trying to sleep on top of an engine boiler. He reports:

We were each apportioned a bed and also an enamel plate and mug, also a knife, fork and spoon, a towel and a piece of ordinary common soap… We put our belongings near our beds as best we could and were then taken down to tea, which was served in a large Mess Room, formerly a store-room. The floor was flagged, while the walls were of bare stone, whitewashed, and the roof of corrugated iron. The tables and forms were of wood, the plainest of the plain. Truly, not a cheery or inviting place in which to dine, but then we were 'rebels' or at least (according to the Internment Order) reasonably suspected of being such desperate characters, and, of course, anything was good enough for us.

The tea, a slight improvement on prison stuff, was poured out of a large bucket and we were each given a quarter of a fairly large size loaf of inferior bread and some tenth rate margarine.

O'Connor, who was later elected Leader of Hut 1, was one of the first to be sent to North Camp, which lay on a slope. He recalls the layout as follows:

The huts were placed oval shape, the w.c.'s (or latrines to use the military term), ablution rooms, bath house and clothes drying room (all very plain structures) being in a straight line up along the centre. The cook-house was at the lower end and was newly erected.

Two lanes ran between the huts and the buildings along the centre. These were named Pearse Street and Connolly Street. There were thirty-five huts, each of which held a maximum of thirty men. Daily routine never varied: life at the camp began at 5.30 every morning when the men were woken by the hooter. They were assembled in order to be counted and then went to wash before breakfast, which was at 7.30. Next came work fatigues for some, which entailed cleaning the huts, dining room, kitchens, latrines, bath house and the YMCA hut. Those on fatigue would then join the rest of the men on the recreation field.

Daily inspection began at 11.00, and involved the Commandant, Adjutant and Sergeant Major. The men were then paraded and were given the opportunity to make complaints or requests. Dinner was at 12.30. O'Connor described the fare as 'a slice of very inferior meat (boiled), soup of a doubtful quality, about half a pound of bad bread and some beans, with a small potato'. The meat ration was eight ounces a day, which included the weight of fat and bones. It was usually frozen Australian or New Zealand meat. Vegetable rations consisted of two ounces per day per man. At 2.00 p.m. the men would again assemble – in the yard in South Camp, or in the field in the North Camp. Tea was at 5.00 p.m. and lights out at 8.20 p.m.

Robert J. Roberts, known as Johnny Roberts, was fifteen when he was employed to run the canteen shop in the camp. In a television interview filmed in 1988 he observed that the men in the South Camp had the greater cause to complain. Two of the dormitories there were in the old malt-house and the granary above it, but the place was so damp that it was shameful. In the interview Roberts stated: 'It was not a place for prisoners. The place was so wet and damp, it was a sin. I felt really bad that the Irish had to sleep in such dampness.'

In 1987, when he was eighty eight years old, Roberts recorded his memories of Fron-goch on tape, a transcript of which is kept at the Meirionnydd Archives at Dolgellau. In the recording he again talks about the dampness that permeated the walls, and about the place swarming with rats. Roberts was also critical of the food that the prisoners were expected to eat, commenting: 'They didn't receive proper food. Black bread and potatoes was the usual fare.' He remembered well the frozen fish

– red herrings – that the men were given. The standard was so bad that the men would throw the food at each other rather than attempt to eat it.

Roberts had spent some time in Liverpool, and his father found him work at the camp within a week of his return. He lived in, sleeping in a hut at the top end of North Camp in barracks set apart for some of the guards and the civilian staff. It included a wet canteen – a bar – which was off limits to the public and, of course, to the internees. He described the part of the canteen where he and another civilian worked as a large, low building 'as long as four bungalows'. He sold cakes and bread. The men would receive a small sum of money for their extras and for goods such as writing paper, tobacco and matches as well as cherry-wood pipes.

These cherry-wood pipes became quite an issue between Roberts and some of the men. Roberts found the Irish to be kind but he found that they were not beyond pocketing the occasional pipe. They would ask the youngster to hand over the box containing the pipes from under the counter so that they could examine them. Then, while Roberts was otherwise engaged, they would pocket some of the pipes and leave without paying.

Roberts complained to the manager, presumably the Camp Commandant. He had no choice. Otherwise he would have had to make up the money for the missing goods. The Commandant, however, ignored the complaint stating that the Irish had their own procedure for dealing with such matters. Roberts therefore went to Collins with his complaint. Collins immediately called the men together, locked the doors and searched them for any misappropriated pipes. Those who had only one pipe each were given the benefit of the doubt, but those with more than one in their possession were ordered to return the extra pipes.

The men were allowed to keep such goods as they could

buy out of the maximum of £1. A Canteen Fund, part of the Central Fund which helped to pay for little extras, was also organised, and food parcels would arrive from families and supporters. These, however, would be opened by the censors, which meant that the contents would have to be eaten immediately or thrown away.

M. J. O'Connor's greatest complaint in North Camp concerned the state of the ground. Following incessant rain and continuous trampling, it turned into red muddy liquid earth:

> The soil was particularly soft and with the disappearance of the grass, mud abounded on all sides. Wherever one stepped, it was the same story – deep liquid mud, which clung to one's boots and soiled hut-floors on which the beds had to be made down each night.

Many complained of wet feet and managed eventually to obtain boots of a more serviceable type from the Military Stores. Clothing too was scanty and of inferior quality; standard issue outfits were known colloquially as 'Martin Henrys'.

Immediately after he arrived, Collins complained about the wet weather in a letter to Susan Killeen. It had rained all the time so that the ground was 'a mass of slippery, shifting mud':

> We sleep 30 in an 'ut (this is the regulation name) the dimensions being 60 long, 16 wide and 10 foot high in the middle. Not too much room to spare! Of course when we've made roads etc. the place will be much better. But the cold at present is – well not too pleasant even now, but I cheer them all up by asking them – what'll they do when winter comes?

Collins' first request to his sister Hannie was for 'a pair of very strong boots, size nine, with nails in them'.

The men were allowed visitors for fifteen minutes once a month. Some of those visiting on a Tuesday would stay on until Thursday, the other visiting day, in order to exchange information – both to and from those in the camp and to others back home. Diarmuid O'Hegarty, who had been released early, was central to the secret information network that was established.

There were some notable visitors to Fron-goch including the Honourable Miss Albina Broderick, sister to Lord Midleton who was a prominent Unionist landowner. Miss Broderick did much good work for the Irish cause, and as a gesture of solidarity changed her name to Irish, and became known as Gobnait Ni Bhrudair. The two Margaret Pearses, mother and sister to Padraig and Willie Pearse, were visitors, as was Mary, sister to Terence MacSwiney. Margaret Gavan Duffy also visited. Her brother George appeared regularly as legal representative to the men in various hearings and was a member of the delegation that negotiated the Treaty.

While many of the men described feeling dismal, Brian O'Higgins detailed the psychological cost of internment. O'Higgins had been Secretary of the Irish College in Carrigaholt in County Clare and was said to have written a poem every day before and after internment under the pen name of Brian na Banban. At Fron-goch, however, writing and even reading was almost impossible. In his memoir, *Laughter Lighted Memories – Humourous Incidents of Ireland's War* he remarks, like others, that the place was teeming with rats, and that he found it impossible to concentrate:

> There is no more deadly, more cruel punishment than the 'freedom' of a prison camp. There is absolutely no privacy. A man cannot say to himself that he will go off and be alone for five minutes. Nerves become frayed, tempers out

of control, and all the little meannesses of man come to the surface. The mind becomes dull, the body enervated, the heart hopeless or hardened, and selfishness displays itself unashamedly in every direction and at all hours of the day.

Men become suspicious, petty, cynical or stupid, their morale is broken down bit by bit, their senses dulled, their best feelings completely submerged. After Fron-goch, whenever I was arrested I hoped that I might be kept under lock and key in a cell rather than be given the 'freedom' and intercourse of my fellows in some hut or dormitory of a prison camp. If I ever had an enemy or opponent whom I wanted to punish or restrain, and had the power to do so, I do not believe I could bring myself to condemn him to a prison camp without his own consent. To my mind it is the most terrible of all humane punishments.

Unlike O'Higgins, most of the men welcomed the comparative freedom of their new home as compared to prison. In a letter to Sean Deacy, Collins wrote: 'There is only one thing to do while the situation is as it is … make what I can of it.'

4
Fron-goch University

Tim Healy MP, who represented various Irish constituencies during his political career, is credited with being the first to describe Fron-goch as the Sinn Féin University. Speaking on the floor of the House of Commons following his visit to the camp in August 1916, he maintained that what Sandhurst was doing to British soldiers, Fron-goch was doing to the Irish Republican Army.

Healy's assertion was picked up by various historians, including Frank O'Connor who writes in *The Big Fellow* that Fron-goch represented one long confrontation between the guards and the internees. From the very beginning it was important that the men were organised, and the internees felt that it was paramount that they, and not the guards, were in control.

W. J. Brennan-Whitmore describes how a General Council of fifty-four men was formed among the internees, a group which included himself and Tomás MacCurtain. The men wasted no time: on the 11th of June, only two days after the camp opened, a Council meeting was held at the communal building, which was named Tara Hall, and the first president, William Ganly from Skerries, was elected. Two Dubliners, Joseph Murray and Thomas F. Burke, were appointed Vice-Presidents; Sean O Mahony, also of Dublin, was appointed Treasurer, and Edward Martin, from Athlone, was made Secretary. An Executive Committee of seven men and various Sub-Committees were also formed, with Tomás MacCurtain, Terence MacSwiney and Brennan-Whitmore among the ten Commandants. Also appointed were thirteen Captains and fifteen Lieutenants. Among the Lieutenants was Richard Mulcahy.

Facing the Council were the camp guards. Some of these officers became legends in the history of the Fron-goch. According to M. J. O'Connor, F. A. Heygate-Lambert, the Camp Commandant, was 'an oldish, cranky-looking man . . . who spoke with a lisp'. He was nicknamed 'Buckshot', after his warning that anyone seen attempting an escape would receive a dose of buckshot.

The Commandant's Adjutant was Lieutenant Burns, a 'cute and slippery' Scotsman and, according to W. J. Brennan-Whitmore, the one officer whom the Irish internees feared. Sergeant Major Newstead, a Welshman, is described by O'Connor as 'a tall, gaunt looking individual of about fifty, with big feet and a fierce-looking moustache'. He was also described as being foul-tempered and foul-mouthed. He warned all new arrivals that any letters, papers, documents and jack-knives that were not handed in would be torn up if found. The absurd image of jack-knives being torn up immediately earned him the nickname Jack-knives. Another officer, a Second Lieutenant, was nicknamed Brimstone because of his fiery character. He could well have been an officer named Grimston, and his surname as much as his nature probably inspired his nickname. Another guard, Lieutenant Bruity, was nicknamed Leatherneck, because of his custom of wearing khaki-coloured rubber collars. There was also Jelly Belly, who 'looked as if he had walked straight out from the pages of Comic Cuts', according to W. J. Brennan-Whitmore.

To all intents and purposes, the camp was run by the officers Burns and Newstead. Gradually, however, it seems that some sort of mutual understanding developed between the internees and the guards and their officers. Séamas Ó Maoileoin describes the ordinary guards as being soldiers who were too old to fight in the war, and when the internees got to know them, they became friendly enough.

There were around four hundred guards at the camp. They

have often been described as members of the Royal Defence Corps, but they were probably forerunners, members of the Home Service Garrison Battalions, as the R.D.C. was not formed until 1917. Johnnie Roberts could recall members of the West Lancashire Regiment among the guards. Later, around sixty members of the Cheshire Regiment arrived from Wrexham, and there is a photograph of kilted members of the Scottish Regimental Guards guarding a large group of Irish prisoners. Joe Good also mentions these kilted guards. The camp guards carried single-shot Martinis during the day and double-barrelled shotguns at night.

Ó Maoileoin describes some of the tricks played on the guards by the internees during the twice-daily head-count. Sometimes internees would furtively move from one line to another, a practice which lasted for a fortnight before the authorities noticed. As a consequence, the lines were separated by ten yards, and armed guards were stationed between the lines.

The guards had their revenge, especially during rainy weather, by deliberately miscounting. This would result in a second and even a third count. The worst offender was an officer nicknamed Rubberjaws.

One officer more than any other frightened the internees. Ó Maoileoin writes that whenever anything went wrong, this officer would fire his rifle into the air. It seemed that the man was suffering from the after-effects of active duty at the front. He was nicknamed the Shaky Officer. Gradually he came to accept the situation and calmed down.

Slowly but surely the internees began to gain the upper hand. Brennan-Whitmore mentions one illustrative incident: the officer nicknamed Brimstone ordered one of the men to stop coughing. As one, all the men began coughing. There was also an attempt to forbid the men the right to wear their Sinn Féin badges. The following day, more men displayed their badges. The guards, knowing that they would lose in this particular confrontation, allowed the badges to be displayed, but not before the Camp Commandant Heygate-Lambert had attempted to impose his authority. He ordered one man to remove his badge but, according to Brennan-Whitmore, the internee stood his ground and challenged the Commandant:

I won't take off my colours and if you or anyone else tries to make me do it, you will want to be a better man than me. You'd better get out of this at once. It's a nice thing for the likes of you to be coming in here and ordering us to take off our little bits of green and yellow and maybe our poor wives and children at home dying. Clear out with yourself now and go and find something better to do.

The Commandant turned white and walked silently away.

The men's stoical attitude towards their situation bewildered the officers. Tom Sinnott of Enniscorthy noted an occasion when Lieutenant Burns taunted them by announcing that they would be confined for life. Immediately, one man stood and shouted, 'Hip-hip ...' Then came the unanimous ear-shattering reply from the rest of the men: '*Hooray!*' Lieutenant Burns shook his head and was heard to mutter: 'I give up,' before he left the building.

One of the greatest problems for the internees was censorship. A Censor named Armstrong was appointed by the Home Office and he would scrutinise every letter that reached the camp. Letters sent by the internees from Fron-goch were diverted to London. Armstrong was a puritanical ex-British soldier, 'a sedate, grey-haired individual' according to M. J. O'Connor. One prisoner named Tierney, who suffered from mental problems, was locked up for a week for daring to use the word 'blast' in a letter. His solitary confinement affected him so much that he had to be transferred to a mental institution.

Later, another Censor was appointed: Lieutenant Bevan, an ex-soldier who had been wounded in the war. He was assisted by some of the prisoners, especially by Tom Pugh, who was one of Collins' men. The internees were allowed to write two letters a week but letters could be refused for the least of excuses.

Séamas Ó Maoileoin recollects a humorous incident when the Shaky Officer confronted him one day with a letter from the prisoner's mother. As it was written in Irish, the officer could not understand it. The same incident is described by Sean O Mahony, and he names the officer as Bevan. Taken together, the two accounts suggest that Bevan and the Shaky Officer were one and the same. Ó Maoileoin recounts how the officer told him that his mother, surely, had not written anything suspicious:

> She is probably urging you to obediently beg for forgiveness for your crimes and to promise to be true to your King from now on and to return to Ireland.

The officer did not realise that Ó Maoileoin's mother was a fierce woman. All three of her sons had fought in the Rising – Ó Maoileoin's brother Tomás was also at Fron-goch – but she was even more militant than her sons. Ó Maoileoin writes:

> He didn't know my dear mother. He was loath to keep my mother's letter from me. He himself had a mother. But rules were rules and he had no translator.

Ó Maoileoin jokingly volunteered to translate the letter himself. To his surprise, the officer agreed, and Ó Maoileoin translated it honestly. Every time he came across a doubtful sentence he pointed it out and the officer would then snip the offending phrase off with a pair of scissors. He ended up with a pocketful of snippets. This was to happen to every subsequent letter Ó Maoileoin either received or sent, and on his release the officer returned to him all the snippets he had removed. On the envelope containing the offending snippets he had written, 'Clippings from the letters of a she-wolf'.

Soon the men lost the right to send their letters in envelopes that were pre-printed with the words 'Prisoner of War'. This was seen as a failure on the part of the internees' General Council. Unfortunately, the men's status as Prisoners of War was diminished by the fact that the Council was run on civilian lines. This fact alone, writes W. J. Brennan-Whitmore, 'abrogated our claim to be treated as Prisoners of War'. Soon the Council was in the hands of senior officers in the Irish Republican Army with J. J. O'Connell made Camp Commandant and Brennan-Whitmore made Adjutant. This led directly to a call by eleven of the men, Brennan-Whitmore, MacSwiney and MacCurtain among them, to establish a military regime among the internees. According to Dorothy Macardle, this was the birth of the Sinn Féin school of thought.

Separate officers were elected for each camp, as follows:

South Camp
Commandant: J. J. O'Connell
Adjutant: W. J. Brennan-Whitmore
Aide de Camp: Captain J. Kavanagh
Provost Marshall: Captain George Geraghty
Quartermaster: Captain Hugh McCrory
Deputy Quartermaster: Captain William Hughes
Medical Officer: Captain Dr Thomas Walsh.

North Camp
Commandant: M. W. O'Reilly
Officers Commanding:
  'A' Co.: Captain J. Connolly
  'B' Co.: Commandant Alf Cotton
  'C' Co.: Captain Liam O'Brien

'D' Co.: Captain Richard Mulcahy
'E' Co.: Captain Robert Balfe
'F' Co.: Captain John Guilfoyle
'G' Co.: Captain Frank Drohan
'H' Co.: Captain Simon Donnelly
'I' Co.: Captain Quinn
'J' Co.: Captain Eamon Price

Elected in charge of dormitories:
Captain Leo Henderson (1)
Commandant Tómas MacCurtain (2)
Commandant Denis McCullogh (3)
Commandant Terence MacSwiney (4)
Captain Joseph O'Connor (5)
Captain Michael Staines in charge of the huts.

From then on the camp was virtually run by the internees. Military training and tactics on military strategies were held under the guards' noses. Brennan-Whitmore became a central figure in this military training, and while in the camp he lectured on guerrilla tactics. In *Portrait of a Revolutionary: Richard Mulcahy* Maryann Gialanella Valiulis emphasises that:

> It was here that Mulcahy experienced the type of organization and solidarity which made prison such an important and radicalizing experience for so many of the prisoners. Basically, the Irish prisoners were in charge of organizing their own living conditions – food, clean-up, recreation, and general discipline. As they considered themselves to be soldiers, they naturally organized along military lines … Prison life was building military skills and increasing ideological awareness.

History has shown what a great mistake it was to herd all the prisoners together in one place. Historians, of course, have the advantage of hindsight, but even as early as during his voyage to captivity Joe Good felt that Britain was allowing the most dangerous of men to escape. In *Enchanted by Dreams* he writes that these survivors were the cream of the Irish Volunteers:

> They compared favourably with professional British army officers; their background and education were, if anything, superior to those of their English counterparts. They were to become financiers, barristers, engineers and industrialists, and achieve eminence in the Irish Free State. These hugely capable young men, who would normally have followed a profession or career, were anything but romanticists, and they were to become the headquarters staff of our active campaign from 1917 to 1921.

In a witness statement to the Bureau of Military History, Thomas Leahy also expressed disbelief at the short-sightedness shown by the British:

> Had the British government known what was taking place under their very own guard and officials, we would have been hunted out of the camp, for it must be realised that men came together in that camp from all parts of Ireland; from towns, villages and places that would have taken years to bring together for the work which had to be done, especially in the training of the army of the Republic.

Séamas Ó Maoileoin thought it a wonderful thing to be receiving military education that was paid for by England, while in his book on Collins, Eoin Neeson describes institutions like Fron-goch as the anvils on which the national amalgam had been forged. This is reiterated by Joe Sweeny:

> We set up our own university there, both educational and revolutionary and from that camp came the hard core of the people who led the subsequent guerrilla war campaign

in Ireland.

Joe Good claims that Fron-goch was a school of revolution, mainly because:

> before the Rising the hardcore of the Volunteer movement had not worked – let alone fought – in close conjunction and comradeship. Fron-goch welded us together, irrevocably.

Good observes that many who had not participated in the Rising were, at Fron-goch, 'infected with the virus of revolution', and describes the varied characters and backgrounds from which they came:

> Men from all parts of Ireland had been sent to Fron-goch. Sallow, tall, sombre men from Galway and the western seaboard; slow to converse, as if suspicious of men from the 'Pale', but true as steel and as implacable against their traditional enemy. Men from the Golden Vale, gay and reckless. Men from Cork, city or county; hard-headed, fiery, touchy and aggressive, with a strong vein of realism. And Dubliners; good natured, improvident and unambitious cosmopolitans.

In her biography of Michael Collins, Margery Forester describes perfectly Britain's gaffe in keeping the men in the same place:

> They were taken from their prisons and spilled together in a vast concourse from North, South, East, and West such as the most nationally-minded could never have hoped in their wildest dreams to have gathered together in Ireland.

Such a cross-section of men from very diverse backgrounds could easily have led to differences of opinion and to disharmony, but despite the 'higgledy-piggledy' sweeping up of men from the four corners of Ireland, W. J. Brennan-Whitmore could not remember a single quarrel occurring among the men.

As little or no discord existed, it was in the British interest to create it. The German connection was a topic of much thought and conjecture from early on. The British guards had heard of Casement's attempts to secure German aid for the Rising, and the British authorities had made much of this both in Britain and Ireland in order to alienate public opinion during wartime. At Fron-goch there were many rumours about the rebels hoarding German gold. It was natural for the guards, therefore, to think that the occasional secret favour could result in a profitable back-hander. The German Plot, which is discussed in Chapter 7, became an excuse later on to arrest a number of Republicans.

The German connection was utilised by Collins at Fron-goch. He realised he could turn the guards' craving for monetary favours to his own advantage. Gaining people's confidence was his forte. His sister Hannie recalled how one warder in particular in Stafford Prison went out of his way to accommodate Collins. It made her wonder if he might have been the first enemy that her brother managed to turn to his side and make a member of his underground army.

The camp officers realised that some of the guards were taking bribes. They thought the solution to the problem was to regularly change personnel, but this did nothing to hinder Collins, even though every new batch of guards was warned against taking bribes. According to Joe Good, the first question asked by some of the new guards was: 'Who's the bloke what's 'anding out the bribes?' Good, who thought Collins could bribe the guards with supreme ease, provides an interesting observation of Collins' shrewd judgement. One day, sitting in the sun watching the guards, he remarked to Joe: 'The nicest thing about the British soldier is his corruptibility.' Joe agreed, adding that the British soldier was the finest flower of English civilisation. Collins replied:

> 'Ah, now that's *just it*. Every "Tommy" takes bribes like a gentleman.'
> 'You mean they're all traitors to their country?'
> 'On the contrary, "Tommy" has such complete confidence in his invincibility of that English "demi-paradise" that he has no compunction about hocking a little of its security to tide him over!'

According to Good, Collins' most significant characteristic was that he never disliked the British:

> If anything, he appreciated and enjoyed them. He was to defeat them in war, and to a large extent around the bargaining table later, *because* he understood them; he could match their manipulative tactics. He'd grown up among them, from his time as a junior civil servant or as an insurance agent in London. Well-educated as he was, with a brilliant analytical mind, he was the first modern Irishman who could match the British military and political leaders.

The guards were not the only ones whose confidence Collins attempted to gain. It was just as important to curry favours with some of the civilian workers both inside and outside the camp. Johnnie Roberts spoke of the many favours he carried out for Collins. Roberts observed:

> Collins must have told his mother about me because she sent me a small present of a tie pin in the pattern of a shamrock inlaid with green Connemara stone for my kindness to her son.

However, as Tim Pat Coogan points out, Collins' mother had died nine years earlier. This does not suggest that Johnnie Roberts was lying but, Coogan claims, Collins had used her name in order to impress the youngster. He tried to make Roberts believe that he was highly regarded.

Roberts described the security measures he had to use, which included him having to show an enamel token every time he entered or left the compound to run an errand. The token was an official pass.

The camp authorities began to suspect that to smuggle out information Collins was using a local farmer who collected pig-swill from the camp. W. J. Brennan-Whitmore denies this categorically, stating that Collins would not have dreamt of using an innocent Welsh farmer in this way. One local farmer who regularly collected pig-swill was Bob Roberts from nearby Tai'r Felin, who later in life became a well-known folk singer. He was openly supportive of the prisoners' fight for their rights. Local people in the Bala area still remember stories of Bob's wife handing out her home-made loaves to the men as they passed on their route marches.

According to Tim Pat Coogan, it was Collins who organised the communications network between the camp and the outside world, and he also reorganised the Irish Republican Brotherhood, which still ruled the roost within the camp:

> The IRB was organised on a cell system, wherein only the cell or circle leader knew who all the members were or how to make contact with the circle above him.... The President of the Supreme Council was the controller, the chief of the entire Brotherhood. Michael Collins was elected Head Centre of the Frongoch outfit.

Coogan also maintains that it might have been in Fron-goch that the first glimmering of another method of warfare, along the lines of de Wet's approach in the Boer War, presented itself.

This was the hit-and run method that the new organisation would come to use, after they abandoned the old tactics used in the Rising. Coogan claims that it was Collins who was the architect of the new method. Marjery Forester goes further, however:

> Senior Volunteer officers in Fron-goch met in secret to receive military instructions and to study suitable strategy and tactics to the requirements of the Irish terrain.... In any future combat, there would be no tall buildings to be held by proud, outnumbered men in uniform; only the lightning stroke, the unseen recoil and reforming before the next blow in another, unsuspected, quarter. Guerrilla warfare was as yet only a growing thought in men's minds. Only the actual necessities of time and place would give it complete shape. In the meantime the rudiments must be mastered. Preparations were made to set up training camps all over Ireland after their release.

According to Forester, Collins was not part of these preparations to begin with, as he held no position in the camp, but with his typical persistence, he demanded the right to attend the various lectures.

It was at Fron-goch as well that Collins earmarked those who would be of use to him in future. When, later, he came to form his group of executioners who would deal with British spies – the ruthless crew named 'The Twelve Apostles' – he chose as members at least six who were ex-Fron-goch internees.

Not all the internees, by any means, were militarily-minded. Some had never been within a mile of a gun. Others were at best lukewarm nationalists. Collins had no time at all for these, and described them as 'Cowards, bloody lousers, ould cods'. It is easy to see, therefore, why some described him scornfully as 'The Big Fellow'.

Fron-goch gave Collins an opportunity not only to plan for

the future but also to muse on the failures of the past. In a letter to Kevin O'Brien written on the 6th of October, he was candid in his opinion of the planning of the Rising. He did not doubt the heroism of those who had died, but he did question the timing. In his opinion, Easter Week was

> ... not an appropriate time for the issue of a memoranda couched in poetic phrases. Nor of actions carried out in similar fashion. Looking at it from the inside (I was in the GPO) it had an air of a Greek tragedy about it, the illusion being more or less completed with the issue of the before-mentioned memoranda. Of Pearse and Connolly I admired the latter the most. Connolly was a realist. Pearse the direct opposite. There was an air of earthy directness about Connolly. It impressed me. I would have followed him through hell had such action been necessary. But I honestly doubt very much if I would have followed Pearse – not without much thought anyway.... On the whole I think the Rising was bungled terribly, costing many a good life. It seemed at first to be well-organised, but afterwards became subject to panic decisions and a great lack of very essential organisation and co-operation.

In the meantime, after the reorganisation of the internees' General Council along military lines, the authorities, aware of the new spirit in the camp, began weeding out those whom they thought were influential, and sent them to English prisons. Among thirty men who were sent to Reading Jail on the 30th of June were MacSwiney, MacCurtain and J. J. O'Connell.

In early August the internees were under a great cloud when the news of Casement's execution was received. Casement had been held in the Tower of London under strict conditions. His guards had been ordered not to converse with him. According to Brian Inglis, the only news Casement received during his time in confinement 'came from a Welsh corporal who whispered to him that there had been a rising in Dublin and that its leaders had been captured and executed'.

But at Fron-goch, life went on. J. J. O'Connell was succeeded as Commandant by Michael Staines. When M. W. O'Reilly was later sent to Reading Jail, he was succeeded by the Commandant of North Camp, Eamon Morkan of Kildare. It is believed that Morkan was the only bank official to have fought in the Rising. For every camp official moved, another would take his place.

Fron-goch was not only a university of revolution in a military sense. An integral part of life at the camp was the educational programme, which involved classes in all kinds of subjects. The Rising has been described as the Teachers' Revolution because so many from the teaching profession had taken part. In Fron-goch, classes were organised from the very beginning and continued despite the comings and goings of the internees. By August these classes were in full swing, with subjects that included Irish, French, Spanish, Latin, Irish History, Mathematics, Book-keeping, Shorthand and Telegraphing.

Thomas Leahy remembered the various classes when he presented his witness account in 1949. He recalled that 'Classes were formed on every subject in everyday life that would be expected of us under the law under the Republic'. He added that they had hoped to be ready to take over departments of government business when it was needed, and the instruction was meant to prepare men to take over these departments when required.

There were also classes in acting, step dancing and public speaking and – according to M. J. O'Connor and Johnnie Roberts – classes in Welsh. Johnnie Roberts was asked to find Welsh language material for the men, following pressure on Colonel Heygate-Lambert from Collins:

I went to Bala, and in Llewelyn Edwards' shop I obtained cards that had been ordered for the infants at the Methodist Chapel. Old Mr Llewelyn Edwards suggested that the wisest move for them if they wanted to set up a class would be to try and obtain *Spurrells Dictionary*, where everything would be in both English and Welsh. And he promised that if Tegid Chapel could do without the cards, we could have them. He also promised a copy of *Spurrells Dictionary* on condition that he was given an order for more – half a dozen copies from Cardiff. And he was. He was given an order for eight copies, so the old man did all right out of it.

Roberts believed that the Welsh language learning materials, including the alphabet card, the dictionaries, leaflets and chalk, were paid for by Collins himself. Whether this was his own money or whether it came from the Central Fund, Roberts did not specify, but he did remember the kitchen being utilised as a classroom because of the warmth, and the tutors using the black-leaded oven as a makeshift blackboard. He reported that one of the Welsh language tutors was Father Stafford, who had some knowledge of Welsh and Gaelic.

Among the Gaelic tutors were Tomás MacCurtain, Richard Mulcahy, Cathal O'Shannon and Séamas Ó Maoileoin. Another was Micháel Ó Cuill, who had walked all the way to Dublin from Sallins in County Kildare to take part in the Rising.

Rex Taylor claims that Collins was inspired to recommence his study of the Irish language, although he never managed to master it and speak it as fluently as native Irish speakers. Later, during the Treaty discussions, Lloyd George deliberately played on the fact that while he was a native Welsh speaker, Collins was not fluent in his own country's language.

The men of Fron-goch not only prepared militarily for the

future, but also prepared for social and financial independence. M. W. O'Reilly had worked in the insurance business in Dublin and, as a Commandant in Fron-goch, he began discussing with other like-minded internees the idea of forming an Irish insurance company. In Ireland, the money market was in the control of British companies.

One of those responsible for forming the company was Denis Mac Con Uladh (McCullough) of Belfast. His idea was to form a company that could compete with the foreign monetary establishments that controlled Irish finance. He wanted to see native institutions motivated by national aspirations and run by the Irish: the aim was to free Ireland economically as well as politically.

Sinn Féin had for a long time taken the same philosophical position, and had argued that Ireland should not be bled dry by a monopoly of foreign interests that profited, at the expense of the Irish, by investing their profits outside Ireland. O'Reilly's plan was supported by Michael Collins and James Ryan.

The New Ireland Assurance Collecting Society, which was established in 1918, was the kind of enterprise welcomed by Collins. His goal was not only a politically free Ireland but an Ireland in which its people were free to live a full life as Irish citizens. In August 1922, he noted that Irish people under British rule had left Ireland open to the poison of foreign practices. His great ideal was for the Irish to rid themselves of all English influence.

When Tim Healy described Fron-goch as a Sinn Féin University, it is doubtful whether he realised how apt his description was. He was referring to the military aspect, but Fron-goch was a wholly comprehensive academy with an expansive curriculum ranging from the Irish language to various crafts, from Latin to Business Studies. Nevertheless, despite these serious forms of activities, as we shall see in the next chapter, the men also found time to sing, dance and play.

5
Rebel Songs and Stories

Despite the dreary conditions in the Camp, and their effect on the internees' mental state, they managed to engage in defiant and energetic cultural activities during their months-long imprisonment at Fron-goch.

In his memoir *With Michael Collins in the Fight for Irish Independence,* Batt O'Connor remembers his contingent of internees arriving at Fron-goch singing 'A Soldier's Song', just as they had done earlier, when they were taken into Wandsworth Prison. In *The Soldier's Song: The Story of Peadar Kearney,* Séamus de Búrca maintains that it was Fron-goch that 'made' the song. The song was written by Kearney, Brendan Behan's maternal uncle, and was set to music by Paddy Heaney in 1907. By the end of 1916 it had displaced 'God Save Ireland' as Ireland's national anthem.

Singing and performing became a part of life in Fron-goch. Concerts were held in the canteen on Sunday nights and on special occasions. They were not unlike the gatherings that were held later in Welsh village halls to welcome soldiers home on leave from the Second World War. Among the Irish internees were many talented performers. One of the main organisers was Douglas ffrench-Mullen who, Sean O Mahony claimed, was a great favourite among the Welsh civilian staff.

On the 25th of June, the hundred and eighteenth anniversary of Wolfe Tone's death, an open-air concert was organised on the playing field, and later continued indoors. Twenty performers took part as instrumentalists, singers, dancers and reciters; the concert included a violin selection by Tomás MacCurtain and a violin *obligato* by Laurence Lynch of Enniscorthy. Pearse's oration at the grave of O'Donovan Rossa was presented by Seán Buckley of Dublin, while T. S. Cuffe, another Dubliner, recited 'Padraig Cohoore'. Among the songs were old favourites such as 'Easter Week' sung by Joe O'Doherty, and 'The Hills of Ireland', sung by Jack O'Reilly of Tralee. One song, 'My Dark Rosaleen', which was sung by Paul Dawson Cusack from Granard, was composed by Seán Butterly of Dunleer and arranged by Cathal O'Byrne of Dublin, both of whom were internees. During the concert interval, the men were addressed in Irish by Pádraic Ó Máille of Maam, and in English by Denis McCullough of Belfast.

On the 8th of August, another concert was held. This event was reported in detail in *The Kerryman* on the 26th of August. That night the chairman was Jimmy Mulkerns, who, in the words of Sean O Mahony, appeared 'in the flowing robes of an Oriental', and was introduced by Peadar O'Brien as 'The Rajah of Fron-goch', a nickname that stuck. Before his arrest and internment, Mulkerns had led a troupe of travelling entertainers named Palmer and Rimlock. He was a singer-comedian and wrote songs and poems. (His son, also named James, became a pioneer in the Irish film industry, and produced over four hundred documentaries, including the Oscar-nominated *An t-Oileánach d'Fill* [The Return of the Islander].)

Among the performers that night were Brian O'Higgins, who sang 'Fried Frogs' Legs' and recited 'The Man from God Knows Where'; Barney Mellows, who sang 'The South Down Militia'; a Dublin man, introduced as 'Signor Toomey' and dressed as a big-game hunter, who sang 'My Old Howth Gun', and Michael Collins, who recited 'Burke and Shea'. Other classics performed that night included 'The West's Awake'; 'Clare's Dragoons'; 'Eileen Óg'; 'A Soldier's Song', and 'Join the British Army'. The concert came to a close with the singing of 'A Nation Once Again'.

On the 31st of October, Halloween was held in the YMCA

hut with Irish singing and dancing, various seasonal games and a fancy dress competition. M. J. O'Connor mentions games such as Snap Apple, Bear Race and Diving in Water for Silver. On the 23rd of November, the anniversary of the Manchester Martyrs was celebrated with a concert and the unfurling of a Republican flag that had been made in the camp. The address was presented by J. K. O'Reilly, who composed 'Wrap the Green Flag Round Me Boys'.

The Fron-goch internees included several poets and songwriters. Perhaps the best-known among them was Brian O'Higgins, but they also included Joseph Stanley, who composed 'The Flag of Freedom', 'The Prison Grave of Kevin Barry' and 'The Shoals of Galway Grey'. It was Stanley who wrote 'The Frongoch Roll-Call', a song that described the protest made by the men against the arrest and trial of fifteen hut leaders who refused to acknowledge the identity of one Michael Murphy, who was liable for conscription into the British Army. Fourteen of the fifteen were found guilty and sentenced to twenty-eight days' hard labour. However, they only spent six days in the cells. The song, sung to the tune of 'The Battle Cry of Freedom', is reproduced in full in Sean O Mahony's book, prefaced by the following explanation:

> While the I.R.A. prisoners were interned in Frongoch Camp, a general roll-call was ordered by the British military authorities, with a view of identifying men for conscripting them into the Army. The general body of the men refused to answer the roll-call, with the result that fifteen of the hut leaders were arrested, court-martialled, and the majority were sentenced to a month's imprisonment wit hard labour [sic]. Despite the hardships involved for both leaders and men, the 'identity strike' was entirely successful, and the following lines commemorate the event.

Fifteen forgetful rebels filed into the Frongoch 'clink,'
Shouting out the battle-cry of Freedom,
In a state of blank abstraction –
      of their names they couldn't think,
So they shouted out the battle-cry of Freedom.

Chorus:
Gott strafe the roll-call, hurrah for the 'Mikes,'
Hurrah for the rebel boys that organised the strikes,
For everywhere the roll was called their names they didn't know,
So they shouted out the battle-cry of Freedom.

Chorus: *Gott strafe*, etc.

Now this caused a great commotion,
      but the rebels spent their time
Shouting out the battle-cry of Freedom.
A Court came down to 'sit on' them –
      the function was sublime –
Shouting out the battle-cry of Freedom.

Chorus: *Gott strafe*, etc.

With their speechifying and oratory
      the courthouse knew no rest,
Shouting out the battle-cry of Freedom.
And the history long of Ireland, sure, they rolled it off their chest,
Shouting out the battle-cry of Freedom.

Chorus: *Gott strafe*, etc.

And when the smoke of battle cleared,
      and th' air was free of dust,
Shouting out the battle cry of Freedom,
They got a month's hard labour for their memories to adjust,
And they shouted out the battle-cry of Freedom.

Chorus: *Gott strafe*, etc.

Now, the moral of the story isn't very far to seek,
Shouting out the battle-cry of Freedom,
When you're up against the Sassenach, don't turn the other cheek,
But shout out the battle-cry of Freedom.

Chorus: *Gotte strafe*, etc.

There was no shortage of artists in the camp and dozens of drawings of various features of Fron-goch have survived. Both W. J. Brennan-Whitmore and Sean O Mahony reproduce a number of them in their respective books. Among the artists whose works from Fron-goch have survived are Michael O'Ceallaigh, Patrick Ronan, Nicholas Murray, Frank O'Kelly (P. Ua Ceallaigh), Cathal MacDowell, Eoghan Ó Briain, Liam O'Ryan and G. Purcell. Other Fron-goch artists included T. Kain, Patrick Lawlor, J. Healy, A. de Courcy, Samuel Hall and James O'Neill.

Several crafts were practised there and, like the drawings, many examples have survived. Bones were carved into all kinds of ornaments, and metal brooches, rings and clay pipes were also fashioned. Even items of clothing have survived. Many of these can be seen at the National Museum and at O'Connoll School Museum in Dublin. One of the most productive craftsmen was Domhnall Ó Buachalla; he presented a collection of his carvings to the National Museum of Ireland. Joe Good remembered some of the men making rings out of coins, and sculptures out of bones: 'Some larger meat-bones became astonishing sculptures,' he comments. 'In one instance, an immense bone became a Celtic cross.'

Among the exhibits at O'Connoll School is a harp carved by John P. Kerr, a clay pipe with a harp emblem made by James O'Leary, and a macramé bag made by Peter Coates. In Kilmainham Jail there is a holy water font with a Celtic cross made by one of the Fron-goch internees.

Reading, of course, took up a considerable amount of the men's time. Family and friends would send books but these would be diverted to London to be censored. In a letter to Alfie Byrne MP, written on the 10th of October, Michael Staines complained about books simply disappearing – books that were sent to the internees were being stolen. Some of these reappeared in a second-hand book stall in Farrington Street in London's East End. Among the books that were lost were a New Testament in Irish sent to Brian O'Higgins, *Seríbhisí Mhicíl Breatnaigh* for Michael Collins, and *Notes of an Irish Exile* for W. J. Brennan-Whitmore.

The men had their own library, and Henry Dixon, one of the oldest internees in the camp, acted as librarian. In a letter to his sister Hannie, Collins was complimentary about the library: he wrote that it wasn't bad, although it contained an odd collection, including books by Robert Service, Swinburne, Shaw, Kipling, Conrad, Chesterton, and 'lots of Irish broadsheet stuff'. Collins' own favourite at the time was Thomas Hardy's *Jude the Obscure*. He asked his sister to send him a copy of *Punch* magazine.

Some newspapers would arrive in the camp from the outside world: Sean O Mahony lists *The Times* (three copies), *Daily Sketch* (six copies), *Daily Mail* (eighteen copies), *Daily Chronicle* (three copies), *Daily News* (twelve copies), and three copies each of the *Yorkshire Post*, the *Manchester Guardian* and the *Morning Post*. Later the *Irish Independent* was added. O Mahony claims that the newspapers were supplied by W. H. Smith for 2s 5½d, but Johnnie Roberts remembered Foyles as the suppliers.

Some banned papers would find their way to the camp, and the men also produced their own papers, which had titles such as *The Daily Rumour*, *The Daily Wire* and *The Frongoch Favourite*.

Publishing posed no difficulty, as there were a number of printers and journalists among the internees. Dick McKee, for example, was a printer, and Joseph Stanley later became Managing Director of the *Drogheda Argus*. Cathal O'Shannon was editor of *The Voice of Labour* and Liam Ó Briain wrote for *New Ireland* (he later became a lecturer in Romance Languages at Galway University). William Sears was editor of the *Enniscorthy Echo* and Paddy Cahill, the Kerry football player, wrote regularly for the *Kerry Champion*. There was also J. J. Scollan, a Dubliner who became editor of the *Hibernian* and later wrote for the *Irish Independent,* while P. J. Doris was editor of the *Mayo News.*

One journalist who could have avoided internment was Michael Knightly: a British officer recognised him among the men at the General Post Office on Easter Monday, and remarked: 'Of course, you are here as a journalist.' When Knightly replied: 'No, I'm here as a soldier of the Irish Republic,' he was immediately arrested.

As in many communities at the time, the barber shop became a natural meeting place. It was here, a place where stories were told, that the unofficial newspapers were organised. According to Séamas Ó Maoileoin, there were two barbers at Fron-goch: James Mallon from Dublin, and Sweeney Newell from Galway. Ó Maoileoin claims that Mallon was one of the most important men in the camp. Not only was he a barber, but he could also heal any disease to do with the hair or the skin. It was said that by using Liffey water he could grow hair on a bald man. After his release from the camp, he went back to his shop on Eden Quay next to Liberty Hall, where he advertised himself as 'The Fron-goch Barber'.

Newell was a blacksmith as well as being a fine barber. According to Ó Maoileoin, he was a large, shrewd man and nothing pleased him more than shocking the English with terrible tales about Ireland. On one occasion, an officer called in and was very complimentary about the shop and the service.

He asked Newell if he would give him the occasional shave. Newell told him he would be delighted to have him sit in the barber's chair, and invited him to do so. The man waited as Newell stropped his cut-throat razor and began to tell stories about killings in Ireland. He boasted that he himself had killed three men while playing hurling. Two of them had been killed accidentally, he said, but the third one had asked for it. He then proceeded to shave one side of the officer's face. The officer asked him what was to become of the other side of his face. The barber told the officer that it was safer to shave just the one side, and he then started shouting about how he hated the English, and threatened to cut the officer's throat. The officer screamed and ran away. He called for one of the guards, telling him that Newell had gone berserk. The guard knew Newell's penchant for such joking. The officer never called again.

The tariff for the barbers' services were as follows: a penny for a shave, tuppence for a haircut, threepence for a haircut with hair oil, and likewise threepence for a bath.

At Fron-goch, self-created entertainment was important for the men not only to relieve the boredom but also to lighten their minds. Physical recreation was just as important. This is why the predominately young men who were kept behind the wire welcomed the route marches. According to M. J. O'Connor, these marches covered some four or five miles, and around a dozen such marches were organised towards the end of August. The weather had at last relented and the internees were allowed out to enjoy the natural beauty of the Welsh moors and hills. Although still under armed escort, some of the men had managed to find military pipes and they were allowed to march to the accompaniment of patriotic Irish airs. M. J. O'Connor remembers:

> We were so weak bodily that we were quite tired the first two or three evenings and had to lie down to recuperate for

a short time. The need of walking exercises was the greatest among our many wants and its absence had a bad effect on the men, a big number getting bloated and suffering from indigestion troubles.

If initially the route marching was difficult for the internees, it was much worse for the guards. Most of them were much older than their prisoners, and they found it difficult to cope with such energetic activity. Ambrose Byrne could remember some of the internees carrying the guns of the tired guards in order to lighten their loads. On one occasion, when a shortage of guards led to the cancellation of one of the marches, a Lieutenant Lambert volunteered to take the men out on his own. A promise from the men not to try and escape would have been good enough for him, but his offer was refused by the authorities.

Collins in particular took to these marches enthusiastically. The various sports that were organised by the internees under the Gaelic Athletic Association rules must have pleased him even more. The GAA had been founded in 1884 to promote Gaelic sporting activities. When the Volunteers were first organised, GAA members flocked to the ranks.

Gaelic football was especially popular at Fron-goch, but hurling was banned because of the danger that the sticks – the *camáni* – could be utilised as weapons. The same prohibition was later ordered at Long Kesh and Magilligan prisons.

The playing field at Fron-goch was naturally named Croke Park, after the famous stadium in Dublin. The games were organised by Dick Fitzgerald, who had captained Kerry when the team became all-Ireland champions in 1913 and 1914. He was one of three county captains at Fron-goch. Sean O Mahony names a host of athletic stars among the men at the camp, including Frank Burke (Proinsias de Búrca), Bill Flaherty, Frank Shouldice, Brian Joyce, Paddy Cahill, Séamus

Dobbyn, Stephen Jordan, Billy Mullins, M. J. Moriarty, Seán O'Duffy, Benny McAllister and Michael Collins. These were stars before they arrived at Fron-goch.

Burke had been a student at St Enda and went on to win All-Ireland Championship medals both in football and in hurling. Shouldice had played football for Dublin before being interned. Joyce had also been a St Enda student and had played football for Dublin. Cahill had played for Kerry and was later elected TD for Fianna Fáil. Dobbyn had played hurling for Antrim.

Séamas Ó Maoileoin confirms that football under GAA rules was the main game played at Fron-goch, and according to Batt O'Connor, Michael Collins was a regular participant. Ó Maoileoin recalls that:

> Two games a day would often be played with the guards watching bemusedly. Having been locked up for some time without much opportunity to stretch our legs, I suppose you could say that we were rough types.

One guard was overheard saying, 'If this is what they're like at play, they must be hellish in a scrap.'

The competition involved three teams from South Camp and one from North Camp fighting it out. The North Camp teams and two of the South Camp teams were named after the leaders of the Rising, but the third South Camp team was a motley crew who had been put together by Dick Fitzgerald. Of Fitzgerald, Ó Maoileoin remarks:

> He was laughed at because they were the bottom of the barrel, while the other teams were made up of the cream of Ireland's footballers. But he was allowed to continue for the fun of it. I was among these 'remnants'. Other than two or three who were hurling men that had never played football before, we were mostly short men. But Dick was a master of

the game and he taught us every trick in the book.

Because of their small stature, the team of no-hopers was known as the 'Leprechauns'. The three South Camp teams played each other twice. The Leprechauns won, and went on to play – and beat – the representatives from North Camp. Ó Maoileoin comments:

> There was never half as much spirit, fun and energy seen in the All Ireland Finals as that which was displayed at Frongoch. Although Dick Fitz wasn't as energetic as he had been five or six years earlier, I'm sure he played better at Frongoch than he had ever done at Croke Park. He was as cunning as a fox.

In June the Wolfe Tone Tournament was held in the camp. A national tournament of the same name was held annually in Dublin. According to Billy Mullins, the two finalists at Fron-goch were the camp versions of County Kerry and County Louth. This microcosm of the game was the only time that an all-Ireland final was held in Wales. The two formal clubs, County Kerry and County Louth, had met three seasons earlier in another tournament, the Railway Shield, and managed to reach the final. Teams representing the four provinces of Ireland also played.

It has been argued that rugby was played at the camp and indeed a rugby ball from Fron-goch is displayed in the National Museum in Dublin, but M. J. O'Connor and Frank Burke were adamant that only GAA rules existed in the camp. O'Connor mentioned other games that were played, such as baseball, skittles and weight-lifting.

Fron-goch's chief sporting occasion was the athletics day on the 8th of August. Collins won the 100 yards sprint in a race that has entered the realms of mythology. M. W. O'Reilly, North Camp Commandant, was leading easily until Collins overtook him in the last few yards. Collins' taunt as he passed O'Reilly was: 'Ah, you whore, you can't run!'

Collins' winning time was recorded as just under 11 seconds, a feat that was quoted in the House of Commons to refute the charge that the prisoners were under-nourished. A Major R. P. Newman quoted Collins' time as $10\frac{3}{4}$ seconds. In a letter to his sister Hannie, Collins indignantly corrected the time to $10\frac{4}{5}$ seconds. Collins came second in the shot-put, however: it was won by Seán Hales, the Munster shot-put champion.

Joe Good recalls getting an interesting insight into Collins' character one night:

It was during the late dusk of evening and long into the night. Mick was trying his best to put a fifty-six pound shot-weight over a bar, a height over which the same shot had been thrown very easily by a strong Galwayman earlier that day. Mick tried and tried – thinking himself alone – and at last he got it over. Then, seeing me there watching him, he said, 'and what do *you* think of that?'

Good replied that he had wanted to see Collins break his neck. They both laughed, and Collins gave Good a bear hug.

Collins' favourite pastime was impromptu wrestling. Gaining the upper hand was not enough for him: he would not be satisfied until his teeth found one of his opponent's ears. Batt O'Connor observes:

In Fron-goch he was full of mischief. Wherever he was, there were always ructions and sham fights going on. Mock battles took place between the men of his hut and those of the adjoining one.... He was all energy and gaiety.

In sport as in other diversions, the men would organise their own activities. No one was more inventive than a man named

Daly – ironically nicknamed Blackguard Daly, because far from being belligerent, he was a most benign man. Johnnie Roberts refers to him as Tom Daly, whereas Sean O Mahony only refers to him in this instance by his nickname. If he was indeed Tom Daly, then he was a member of the Irish Citizen Army and had lived in Fairview, Dublin.

South Camp was overrun with rats and it was a constant source of bitter amusement to the internees that the Irish word for rat is 'francach', a word not very different from 'Fron-goch'. One of Daly's pet diversions was to catch these rats in baited traps, and Johnnie Roberts, the fifteen-year-old Welsh camp worker, never forgot either Daly's method of catching them or what he subsequently did to them. According to Roberts, Daly was over six feet tall and had Dracula-like teeth. He would remove the rats from their traps, place them in a sack and gas them using a sulphur candle. The dead rats were then cremated in the boiler room.

Sometimes, however, a rat would be spared temporarily and used as an unwilling star in what became known as 'Daly's Circus'. Benches were placed in the compound, and when the audience was assembled, Daly would produce the biggest rat he could find. Wrapping a sack around his hand, he would force the rat into an old army sock and another man would tie a length of string to the creature's tail. Roberts recalls:

> He would then allow the rat to crawl beneath his clothes. Then he would reveal the rat's bite marks all over his body. The show would end with Daly pulling the rat out of the sock and biting the creature's head off as blood poured down his chin.

Roberts, as an outsider, felt privileged to be invited as a spectator to 'Daly's Circus'. He felt it proved to him that he had been accepted by the men.

Many commented on the rat infestation. In a letter to Susan Killeen, Collins wrote that he had woken up to find a rat nestling between his blankets.

One pastime that became popular was called 'Dead Man' and was devised by Joe Good, who described the rules as follows:

> One man stood in a circle of others, stiff as a mummy, and allowed himself to be pushed across the circle from one side to the other; he who failed to catch and return the body became 'Dead man'. This adventure provided indoor exercise and amusement and needed a certain amount of nerve.

Johnny Roberts remembered the men playing pitch and toss, and draughts, chess and card games were also played, but playing cards for money was banned after a memo was sent around by Captain W. J. Brennan-Whitmore, who declared in no uncertain terms that gambling would 'besmirch our beautiful ideals'.

Surely the most bizarre pastime was the Irish Fair, which was enacted by the internees during rainy weather. Brennan-Whitmore describes the shenanigans:

> Quite suddenly one wet morning as the crowd stood huddled under the archway, bulls began to bellow, cows to low, sheep to bleat, pigs to squeal, and horses to neigh and champ. Dogs barked furiously from various quarters, and the strident voices of buyers and sellers rose in bellicose bargaining. The effect was wild and ludicrous.

At Fron-goch 'Craobh na Sróine Dierge', a branch of the Gaelic League, was formed to support the Irish classes. The name was a translation of 'The Red Nose Society'. It was mistakenly believed that this name was a translation of

Fron-goch, but Fron-goch means 'red breast', and refers in this case to a local topographical feature.

A society called 'The Black Hand Gang' was also formed in Fron-goch. Starkly differing opinions about the group have been expressed. Some, like Joe Clarke, believed it to be a crew of pranksters, while others thought it a serious secret society from which Collins took the idea of 'The Twelve Apostles', or 'The Squad', which was formed in September 1919 with the purpose of assassinating spies. At Fron-goch, Domhnall Ó Buachalla was a prominent member of 'The Black Hand'; he was later elected TD for Kildare and went on to become Ireland's last Governor General.

The internees were almost a hundred percent Catholic. Sean O Mahony lists only five Protestants among them: Arthur Shields, Harry Nichols and Ellet Elmes from Dublin; Sam Ruttle from Tralee and Adare, and Alf Cotton from Tralee and Belfast. Séamus McGowan from Drumcondra, Dublin was also from a family of Protestants. He fought at the GPO and it is said that he was the inspiration for the central character in Seán O'Casey's play *Shadow of a Gunman*.

A hut was set apart for Mass every Sunday and every other week-day, and the men's spiritual needs were catered for at first by an Austrian priest, who might well have been a relic from the time of the German prisoners. He was followed by an English priest and, subsequently, by a priest who would visit from Wrexham. Finally, after Seán T. O'Kelly had managed to smuggle out a letter to the Archbishop of Dublin informing him of the need for a resident priest, the Dublin diocese sent Father Laurence Stafford, a Chaplain to the Forces. He arrived at the camp in military uniform, which provoked taunts and derision from the men. O'Kelly managed to persuade him to wear his priestly robes but W. J. Brennan-Whitmore believed that Father Stafford continued to wear his uniform underneath.

From the beginning Stafford sided with the authorities and

began reproaching the men for their sin in taking part in the Rising. Some of the internees went as far as to accuse him of sowing dissent among the men. This led the men either to heckle Father Stafford or ignore him entirely. The Chaplain was described by M. J. O'Connor as a 'natty' little man, and he had his uses. Unbeknownst to him, his bag was used to smuggle in tobacco and secret messages. Whatever his failings, Stafford was still considered by Seán T. O'Kelly to be a good man at heart

The men had their own Amusements Committee, whose members included Joe O'Doherty (who had been captivated by a rendition of 'When will the Day Break for Erin' on his way over on the cattle boat) and the librarian Henry Dixon, who was a prominent IRB man. Arthur Shields was also on the committee: he was the member of the Abbey Theatre who ought to have been on stage on that Easter Monday. Instead he found himself fighting in the GPO. The play was *The Spancell of Death* by T. H. Nally, but unfortunately for the dramatist another greater drama took prominence and his play was never performed. Catherine Rynne describes the play in *The Story of the Abbey Theatre*: 'It was set in eighteenth-century Mayo and dealt with witchcraft, the spancell being a sort of love charm made out of a long strip of skin cut from a corpse.'

Following his release from Fron-goch, Shields went on to appear in some two dozen Hollywood films, including *How Green Was My Valley* in 1941, in which he played the part of the puritanical deacon Mr Parry. He also starred in another Welsh film, taking the part of Mr Davies in Emlyn Williams' *The Corn is Green*. He died in Santa Barbara, California in 1970. (Shields' younger brother, Barry Fitzgerald, became a better known actor. He had fewer films to his name, a mere fifty, but they included classics such as *The Quiet Man*. Indeed, he appeared with his brother in *How Green Was My Valley* as Cyfartha Lewis.)

The Spancell of Death was to have been part of a double bill at the Abbey Theatre. The other play that Easter week was Yeats' classic, *Cathleen ni Houlihan*. Written as a blatant piece of propaganda and first performed in 1902, the main character, an old woman who personified Ireland and called her sons to fight for the cause, was played by Maud Gonne. In his poem 'The Man and the Echo', the narrator, on his death bed, asks:

> Did that play of mine send out
> Certain men the English shot?

Conor Cruise O'Brien's answer was a definite 'yes': the actor who was to have played the part of Peter Gillane was Seán Connolly, a member of the ICA. He was shot dead on the Tuesday afternoon of the Rising at the time when he should have been on stage.

Another Fron-goch internee from the theatre world was John MacDonagh, whose brother Thomas was executed after the Rising. MacDonagh was a theatre manager in 1916, and he went on to work in radio and was later appointed Radio Athlone's Head of Productions (Radio Athlone was the forerunner of Radio Éireann). MacDonagh also wrote a number of children's books and a successful play, *The Irish Jew.*

In the camp, most of the men kept a sort of autograph memorial book, in which they would note personal memories and in which they would also invite their fellow internees and visitors to write a note or a few lines of poetry. Sean O Mahony includes many instances in his book on Fron-goch. Michael Brennan of Clare quotes Lord Fisher of the Admiralty: 'When you go to war, hit hard and hit everywhere.' Richard Mulcahy's contribution speaks volumes about the man: 'The Seed has been sown, the harvest must be reaped.' Matty Neilan, who would go on to represent Galway as TD wrote: 'The language of the conqueror on the lips of the conquered is the language of the slave.'

Two contributions by Terence MacSwiney, the future Lord Mayor of Cork who would die on hunger strike, are revealing. One states: 'No country can be conquered whose sons love her better than their lives.' The second is a quotation from *The Meditation of Christ* by Thomas á Kempis: 'Cease to complain, consider my passion and the suffering of my saints: you have not yet resisted into blood.' Finally, one of Collins' contributions echoes the events of Easter Week: 'Let us be judged by what we attempted rather than by what we achieved.'

6
Trials and Tribulations

On the 1st of December 1916 a 'Special Correspondent' in the *Manchester Guardian* attempted to highlight the fundamental cause of troubles that existed at Fron-goch in an article highly sympathetic to the internees:

> Most of the serious troubles in the camp may be traced to one fundamental grievance of the prisoners – the feeling that they have been wrongly interned and made to undergo these hardships without ever having the chance of defending themselves in a trial.

Almost a year later, W. J. Brennan-Whitmore reproduced the article in *With the Irish in Frongoch* and accused the journalist of being 'entirely astray in his premise'. Correcting the 'Special Correspondent', he notes two specific causes which had led to the troubles:

> Firstly, the refusal of the authorities to keep their undertaking to recognise and treat us as Prisoners of War; and second, the determination of the Irish Prisoners themselves to prevent the conscription of their fellow-prisoners who were liable under the Military Service Act.

In *Michael Collins* Rex Taylor reinforces Brennan-Whitmore's point of view. He describes life in Fron-goch as one long row with the English authorities about the 'refugees'. These 'refugees' were those among the internees who had lived in mainland Britain at one time or another, and who were therefore liable for conscription into the British Army. Conscription, or compulsory enrolment, was introduced by the

British Government in January 1916, but the Bill did not include Ireland. Some sixteen thousand conscientious objectors – known derogatorily as 'conchies' – refused on pacifist grounds to fight. Almost half of these agreed to perform non-combatant roles such as stretcher-bearing. As the war proceeded and the number of casualties grew, attempts were made to include Ireland in the Conscription Bill. The so-called German Plot, detailed in the next chapter, was conceived in order to expedite conscription in Ireland.

Groups of some sixty internees were regularly sent from Fron-goch to London by train to face a tribunal or an advisory committee before a High Court Judge, Lord Justice Sankey, later to become Lord Sankey. This became known as the Sankey Advisory Committee. The internees preferred to call it the Sankey Mock Trial. An appearance in London would normally last two days, during which the men were held at Wormood Scrubs or Wandsworth Prison.

The purpose of the hearings was to establish the men's names, addresses and ages, and the part that each had played in the Rising. The intention was to weed out and identify the sixty or so internees who the authorities suspected had lived in Britain and were therefore liable for conscription. Such hearings could not be described as appeal courts as the men had not even been charged with bearing arms against the Crown during the Rising. After the hearings, some were to be released and others sent back to Fron-goch or to prison. Others were to be conscripted into the British Army – or that, at least, was the plan.

The Sankey hearings were also useful in that they disrupted life in the camp, and thus interrupted the organisation and solidarity among the internees, but every time one of the leaders was removed, another would immediately take his place. The men regarded their London visit as a welcome adventure that brightened the dreariness of the daily routine.

By the 22nd of July, the cases of up to thirteen hundred men had been considered by the Sankey Committee. Of these it was recommended that eight hundred and sixty men should be released. Outwardly this appeared to represent an enlightened attitude on the part of the authorities, but in fact what it indicated was how many Irishmen had been falsely arrested during the Rising.

M. J. O'Connor described his journey to the English capital: starting at 11.00 a.m., he and his fellow-internees travelled through Crewe, Shrewsbury, Wolverhampton and Birmingham and arrived in London at 5.15 p.m. Upon reaching Paddington Station the men were taken to jail by bus.

The internees were only given three or four minutes to answer the committee's questions. They were represented by George Gavan Duffy, who had been a member of Sir Roger Casement's defence team. The men naturally believed that the main purpose of these hearings was to collect information about their part in the Rising and, more importantly, to discover whether they were liable for conscription. Consequently they went out of their way to confuse the panel members. Séamas Ó Maoileoin demanded that he should be able to answer in Irish. A translator was called but unfortunately he spoke only Scots Gaelic. A Gaelic-speaking policeman was summoned, so thereafter Ó Maoileoin turned to the Aran Islands dialect that he had been taught by Miceál Ó Maoláin at Fron-goch. Ó Maoileoin was sent back to Wales with the committee none the wiser about him.

The question of military conscription remained a great source of tension. The authorities were unremitting in their attempts to force the 'refugees' among the internees to acknowledge their names. The refugees could see little sense in the authorities attempting to persuade Volunteers to fight for the Crown when just a few weeks earlier they had fought against Britain. They also felt that the conscription of Irishmen who had spent time in Britain constituted a further step towards the establishment of general military conscription in Ireland.

One way of making it difficult for the authorities to identify who among the internees were the refugees was by creating confusion as the internees' names were called during the daily roll-call. Internees would answer to other men's names, and others would refuse to answer at all. Indeed, some of the men returned home under assumed names.

Among the men were some who had deliberately confused the authorities by giving false or misleading names when they were arrested. W. J. Brennan-Whitmore's name, for example, cannot be found in the *Sinn Féin Rebellion Handbook*. Nor does it appear in the list compiled by Sean O Mahony in *Frongoch: University of Revolution*. The reason is that Brennan-Whitmore gave his name as William Whitmore, and it is as William Whitmore that he appears on page 75 of the *Handbook*.

The conscription controversy reached its climax on the 1st of October, when a prisoner called Hugh Thornton challenged the authorities (Thornton was later killed as a Free State soldier during the Civil War, while his brother Frank was active in the Rising and became deeply involved in intelligence work for Michael Collins). Hugh Thornton twice refused to acknowledge his name, and he was surrounded by armed guards with drawn bayonets. The third time his name was called, he decided to comply, and Lieutenant Burns rushed towards him brandishing a cudgel. Thornton kept his head, but he had to face a military tribunal, and was sentenced to two years' jail with hard labour for refusing to join the British army.

The internees were charged with concealing their knowledge of Thornton's identity, and they were all punished for 'gross subordination'. Letters and visits were stopped for a week. When their punishment was announced, however, the men merely shouted their defiance. The authorities now turned to fairer means to persuade them to cooperate. They offered to release the internees on condition that they signed an agreement to keep the peace. This, of course, would involve them acknowledging their names. Only three accepted the offer.

The authorities now reverted to their old underhand methods. Three Liverpool brothers, George, Jon and Pat King, were identified after they signed store chits for clothes. They were charged under the Military Service Act. One of them was subsequently released on medical grounds. The other two were found guilty and imprisoned.

Another ruse used by the authorities was to get the men to sign for letters and parcels. The pressure put upon the refugees was so great that they considered surrendering so as not to cause more difficulty for the non-refugee majority. Collins, however, was adamant that no cooperation would be allowed. Such was the internees' commitment to resisting the authorities' eagerness to identify the refugees that when Tom Daly of Fairview, Dublin was told of his wife's death, he would not identify himself, although he was not himself one of the refugees. The authorities even refused to send a telegram asking his brother to make the necessary arrangements.

One of the worst examples of the authorities' manipulative tactics was the promise made to a man called Fintan Murphy that if he identified himself he would be paroled. Such an offer had been made to the men in general, but this was aimed personally at Fintan Murphy. Murphy refused to rise to the bait, but was later identified and tried under the Military Service Act. Another more absurd tactic was to inform a Michael Murphy that his wife had died and that he would be allowed to attend her funeral if he identified himself. Michael Murphy knew his wife had not died for the simple reason that he was not married. He remained unidentified, but such was the confusion that a man called Barrett was sent to London in his name, and was accused under the Military Service Act. When Barrett appeared before the court, Murphy's father told the authorities that the man in the dock was not his son. Barrett was immediately sent back to Fron-goch.

Colonel Heygate-Lambert, the Fron-goch Commander, was furious, and threatened to leave the camp full of corpses if he could not have discipline from the men. Despite the use of spies and undercover Royal Irish Constabulary officers, few of the men were identified. To add to the chaos, on one occasion some of the men managed to blow all the electrical fuses, and in the ensuing darkness two pipers marched along Connolly and Pearse Streets in the camp playing Irish melodies.

As a result of the refusal to identify themselves, three hundred and forty-two men were sent to the South Camp for punishment, where, according to MP Alfie Byrne 'they were herded in three insanitary, ill-ventilated, badly-lighted grain barns, in which they are locked from 6.15 in the evening until 6.15 in the morning with the loss of all privileges'.

North Camp, which had been almost closed as the number of internees decreased, was still used as a place of punishment, but now effectively became a clearing house for the men whose names were known. Those whose names were not known, and who refused to cooperate, were kept in South Camp.

The game of cat and mouse continued. Liam Pedlar, a man who was already serving punishment, was threatened with being shot for daring to greet the ration party who were delivering food from North Camp. James Grace was arrested and sentenced to fourteen days on bread and water for refusing an order. He went on hunger strike and was released back into the camp at the insistence of the camp doctor.

One event occurred that was to have widespread repercussions sixty years later. Some prisoners who were serving out their punishment in the South Camp for failing to identify themselves refused to wear clothes and went around wrapped in blankets or, as Brennan-Whitmore described it, 'wrapped a-la Red Indians'. This was the first occurrence of Republican prisoners 'going on the blanket' and it would be repeated in Long Kesh and Magilligan in 1976. At Fron-goch the protest was made in jest, while at Long Kesh and Magilligan it was an expression of the far more serious refusal to wear the prison uniform worn by criminals.

The Michael Murphy affair, in which Barrett had been sent to a hearing in London in his name, continued to simmer. It eventually led to fifteen hut leaders being court-martialled even though they were not enlisted soldiers or liable for conscription. They included Richard Mulcahy, Tom Sinnott, Frank Shouldice and Seán MacMahon. They were defended by George Gavan Duffy, who had defended some of the internees at their Sankey trials. All but one were found guilty of contravening the Military Service Act and were sentenced to twenty-eight days' hard labour within the camp. The authorities had demanded that the hearings should be held *in camera*, but reporters on the *Manchester Guardian* and the *Irish Independent* were allowed to attend. This meant that the hearings were held outside the confines of the Camp, in Colonel Heygate-Lambert's house. The hearings led to widespread publicity, and after six days in the punishment cells the men were allowed to return to normal camp life.

Eventually the authorities met with partial success and identified three men among the internees who were liable for conscription into the army. Seán Nunan was sentenced to a hundred and twelve days, his brother Ernest to six months and Thomas O'Donoghue to four months, again under the Military Service Act. All three sentences included hard labour. With this partial success, the authorities gave up their attempts to identify the remaining refugees among the internees.

Apart from the conscription issue, the other source of conflict at Fron-goch was the issue of work allocation. The internees were willing to undertake any labour that would maintain their day to day existence. Cleaning their own huts or dormitories, for example, was acceptable, as was maintaining the roads within the camps – for which work they were allocated $1\frac{1}{2}$ pence per hour. Such work was also physically beneficial.

On the 1st of October, however, the authorities tried to persuade the internees to undertake quarrying work at the Arenig granite workings, which lay a few miles away. For this work they were to be paid $5\frac{1}{2}$ pence per hour. From their weekly pay, a sum of seventeen shillings and sixpence was to be deducted for the cost of their transport by train, and for maintenance at the camp. The men refused, noting that they would also be depriving local people of much-needed work. Their refusal was strengthened by a hunger strike. The hunger strike over work would not be the last in which the internees engaged.

The internees were also urged to undertake agricultural work on local farms, just as the German POWs had done. One of the men, Barney O'Driscoll, commented that he and the others would have been only too happy to work salvaging Irish crops. They would have beeen more than willing to work on their own native land.

It is unclear whether in fact the internees did undertake some work outside the camp. In the 1987 documentary on Fron-goch by *Ffilmiau'r Nant,* Morris Roberts, who lived at nearby Tai'r Felin, recalled his father Bob Roberts mentioning that the men had been involved in felling trees at the warren above their farm. However, as the men refused to undertake any work outside the camp, it is possible that they were merely returning from a route march, and Roberts mistook this for them returning from work. As they came past the mill kept by the Roberts family they would fill their caps with flour. 'They were almost starving,' Morris Roberts reported. 'That's the impression I was given.'

Bob Roberts' sympathies were entirely with the internees. He told his son Morris:

Unlike the Germans, the Irish were treated like swine. They were shown no respect and as a result they showed no discipline. They were in a filthy condition and neglected. And almost starving.

Johnnie Roberts, the teenager who worked in the camp, could remember the quarry incident, when the men's refusal to work led to a hunger strike. Morris Roberts also recalled the hunger strike, and that the authorities refused the internees any medication until they abandoned their protest.

Fasting has long been a Celtic method of exerting pressure on authority. The 'Troscad' and the 'Cealacha', which means fasting on or against a person or achieving justice by starvation, was practiced in the Middle Ages and earlier as a legal form of redressing a grievance. In *The Druids* Peter Beresford Ellis explains:

Under law, the person wishing to compel justice had to notify the person they were complaining against and then would sit before their door and remain without food until the wrongdoer accepted the administration or arbitration of justice.... It is fascinating, as well as sad, that in the long centuries of England's sorry relationship with Ireland, the Irish have continued a tradition of the *troscad* which has become the political hunger strike. One of the most notable Irish political hunger strikes was that of the Lord Mayor of Cork, Terence MacSwiney, also an elected Member of Parliament, who was arrested by the English administration in Cork City Hall and forcibly removed from Ireland to

London's Brixton Prison.

M. J. O'Connor recalled what became known as the Ash Pit Incident when, on the 13th of September, the men were ordered to move and empty the guards' refuse bins, which stood in an area outside the compound. Collins also described this incident and the quarry dispute in a letter to his sister Hannie on the 25th of August:

It is a custom to appoint a fatigue of 8 men every day, for general scavenging & removing ashes, inside the wires. About 8 or 10 days ago the particular party that was on for the day was ordered outside the wires to do scavenging &c for the soldiers. Of course they refused. They were immediately sent to cells and since then have been imprisoned in the northern portion of this camp being deprived of their letters, newspapers, smoking materials. Every day since 8 men have been given the same treatment, & the affair still goes on.

The number of men punished in this way gradually grew to a hundred. They were confined to their huts for five hours every day, deprived of parcels that were sent to them, and were restricted to writing one letter per week. Collins remarked to his sister: 'This practice of confining to cells for trivial things is a thing which the commandant glories in.'

Following the publication of a letter in the *Irish Independent* that revealed these punishments, the authorities decided on the 9th of October to end them.

The low standard of the camp food also had a detrimental effect on the men. In that same letter to Hannie on the 25th of August Collins noted: 'With the exception of Friday when we get uneatable herrings, the food never varies, meat quite frequently and dried beans are the staple diets. The potato ration is so small that one hardly notices it.'

Much of the ill health that the men suffered was blamed on the scarcity of fresh food. This led to many cases of scurvy. Sciatica and tuberculosis were also common. When one of the men, Maurice Fitzsimons, was taken to hospital suffering from appendicitis, he was deprived of his clothes, and had to make his way to the toilet naked.

On the 20th of November, an internee named Tierney suffered a complete breakdown. He was so terrified of conscription that he went mad. He was kept in an isolation hut, where he was tended by eight comrades. Four more internees subsequently broke down. Christopher Brady from Dublin contracted TB, and he died from its effects two months after his release. He was twenty-seven years old. Jack O'Reilly suffered from acute anaemia and died the following year. He was given a military funeral. Thomas Stokes of Enniscorthy also died of an illness caught at Fron-goch. The fourth, William Halpin of Dublin, suffered so much from depression that he tried to slit his own throat. After the camp was closed, he was moved to Grangegorman Mental Hospital in Dublin, where he later died.

Two others are known to have suffered mental problems at the camp. One, Daniel Devitt (named as Davitt in local newspapers), caused quite a stir by disappearing from the camp on the 4th of August. The authorities believed he had mingled with a crew of seventy-nine internees who were released on that day and who had travelled by train through Chester to Holyhead. However, it was revealed in *Y Seren* on the 26th of August that Devitt had been arrested between Bryneglwys and Llandegla, some twenty-five miles from Fron-goch, three days after his disappearance. Samuel Edwards, a local postman, had seen him walking along the road and had called the police. Superintendent Morgan from Bala and Sergeant Lloyd of Corwen soon arrested Devitt, but it emerged that he was not an escapee: he had suffered a mental breakdown and had simply walked out of the camp unchallenged.

There are no records of any internee escaping from Fron-goch or even attempting to escape. For the committed Republicans there was more to be gained from remaining there while preparing for future action. However, there is an anecdote told in Connemara about a girl from Bala who fell in love with an internee named Pádraic Ó Máille. The girl, dressed as a priest, helped Ó Máille escape, but he is said to have been arrested shortly afterwards and interned elsewhere.

In addition to scurvy, TB and mental breakdown, there was also a bad outbreak of German flu in the camp at the beginning of November. Those who were already weak from their hunger strike protest were particularly vulnerable, as protesting internees were also refused the right to medical treatment.

The effect of the lack of nutrition on the internees, and the authorities' order that those who refused to answer to their names should not have medical treatment deeply affected the camp medical officers, Dr David Peters and his nephew, Dr R. J. Roberts. They ran their own doctors' practice, but also visited the camp on a daily basis between 10.00 a.m. and 12.00. Initially they adhered to the authorities' ruling, and this led to accusations by the internees of professional misconduct. Increasingly, the doctors were caught between following the authorities' rules and the Hippocratic Oath, which protects the right of everyone without exception to receive medical attention.

It all became too much for Dr Peters. On the 14th of December, Heygate-Lambert announced to the internees that Dr Peters had taken his own life, and that they were answerable to God for what had happened. This infuriated the internees, because they knew very well that it was the Commandant who was primarily responsible for the unfair burden that had been placed on the doctor's shoulders. M. J. O'Connor asserts:

This was a terrible allegation to make, and naturally found sudden and indignant resentment. There were loud cries of 'liar' on all sides, mingled with shouts of 'you were responsible yourself'; 'what about the men sent to the Asylum?' etc. The Commandant did not count on this and was in a quandary as to what to do. Believing discretion the better part of valour he walked off with the Adjutant and Sergeant Major, continuing his round of inspection. He did not come near us again that day.

O'Connor described the sorrow that the men felt about Dr Peters, and described him as a kind, humane man, who was spoken well of by those men whom he treated. He performed his professional duties in a quiet, unostentatious way and won good opinions of everyone in the camp.

According to O'Connor, on the day after the announcement of Dr Peter's death, when the command 'hats off' was given at inspection, the men refused to uncover their heads, as a protest against the Commandant's allegations. O'Connor's assessment of Heygate-Lambert's behaviour is scathing:

> The Commandant was, without the shadow of a doubt, responsible for the worry caused Dr Peters for had he (the Comdt.) not sent prisoners to the South Camp under punishment in the worst and most unhealthy dormitories in the Camp there would not be so much sickness and consequently no overwork for Dr Peters. Furthermore the fact that Dr Peters saw scores of men suffering through no fault of their own, and that he was not allowed to attend to them, preyed to a great extent on his mind and worried him, kind, considerate man that he was....
>
> All this could have been prevented by the Commandant, had he so willed, but the various dealings with that gentleman showed him to be what he really was, an unfeeling, dogged type of Englishman whose whole

object seemed to be to deal with men as if they were so many serfs, impose on them, for the mere purpose of exercising his little powers, whatever orders his fancy at the moment prompted him and then do his utmost to have these orders obeyed, regardless of their utility and the suffering caused those who did not carry them out as they did not see any purpose they could possibly serve.

According to O'Connor, Heygate-Lambert's attitude made everyone in the camp – even the soldiers – dislike him. His 'iron heel' methods were hated by all, 'but he came up against a tough opposition when he came in contact with Irish prisoners. Some of the soldiers often said that had they disobeyed orders as we had, they would get two years' imprisonment at least.' O'Connor also pointed out that the Commandant's allegations were the worse for having been made before the Coroner's inquest had been held.

Joe Good described Dr Peters as a victim of circumstance, torn between military orders, Republican propaganda and the expectations and pressures of his own profession. His death had such an effect on Michael Collins that Collins wrote to Heygate-Lambert and to the Home Office emphasising that the men had never meant any harm to the doctor and that he was much grieved by his death.

On December 23rd the local Welsh language newspaper *Y Seren* described Dr Peters' death as having left a huge gap in the community in which he had served. Peters was the son of a well-known local family, and had worked as assistant to two local doctors before qualifying. He had spent fourteen years living in the locality and was a deacon in the chapel. According to the obituary, Peters was a quiet, unassuming man who kept himself to himself and loved contemplation and solitude. He was a writer and poet who adjudicated in local literary competitions, and was a compassionate and conscientious doctor.

The same edition of *Y Seren* also published a report on the inquest into Peters' death. Dr Peters' widow testified that his health had not been good for some time and on the eve of his death had spent a restless night and had suffered severe headache.

PC Jones, a local constable, had discovered Peters' body on the Thursday morning in the Tryweryn river, just below the railway bridge. Dr R. J. Roberts, Dr Peters' nephew who assisted him at the camp, testified that his uncle had been disturbed by 'sad and unfounded reports made by Irish prisoners'. Dr Roberts had tried to cheer him by saying that Peters would be able to answer to such accusations without any problem. He suggested Peters should leave for Corwen, where he also practiced, and leave everything to him (Roberts). Peters had been there on the Monday and Tuesday and was met at the station by Roberts on the Wednesday morning where they discussed whether it would be wise for Peters to return to Corwen. He had not seen him alive again. Roberts testified that his uncle tended to lean to one side, and he was of the opinion that this might have made him topple towards the river. After the Coroner's summing-up, the jury returned a verdict of 'suicide while the balance of the mind was disturbed'.

The issue of Dr Peter's death was raised in Parliament, and was perhaps a catalyst for change in the internees' situation, coming as it did after several months of mounting public pressure about camp conditions. Not all of that public attention had been welcomed by the internees themselves, however.

As knowledge of camp conditions trickled out to the outside world, Irish politicians realised there was political capital to be made through pleading the internees' cause. One of these was John Redmond, who had previously condemned the Rising. He was leader of the Irish Parliamentary Party, the party that had cheered Prime Minister Asquith's announcement on the 3rd of

May that three signatories of the Republican Proclamation had been executed.

The newly-elected MP and Dublin Alderman Alfie Byrne visited Fron-goch, while as early as July two MPs for Kerry, Tom O'Donnell and Michael Flavin, had pledged their support for the men. O'Donnell went as far as to boast through the press that his intervention could hasten the Kerry men's release. The internees from Kerry responded by writing a letter to *The Kerryman* newspaper announcing that not a single internee had asked for O'Donnell's support. The letter appeared on the 15th of July. According to M. J. O'Connor, only two internees from Kerry refused to condemn the statement by the MPs, and one of the two was related to Flavin through marriage.

Flavin managed to obtain permission to visit the camp but afterwards was accused by the men of releasing misleading reports about the men's response. He tried to earn the men's favour by offering them baskets of food for their journeys to the Sankey hearings. One internee, Dan Healy, received cigarettes, tobacco and sandwiches from Flavin at Paddington Station. Flavin suggested that as the food had been prepared at the House of Commons perhaps Healy wouldn't eat it. Healy replied: 'We're so hungry we'd not eat only the sandwiches but the Speaker himself.' Flavin later renounced the Parliamentary Party's stance on the Rising and endorsed Sinn Féin.

In a similar case to that of the MPs for Kerry, the Bandon Town Commissioners in County Cork also called for the release of the internees. In a letter to the *Southern Star* Corkmen at Fron-goch rejected their support.

One notable exception to those politicians who jumped on the wagon for their own gains was the North Roscommon MP Larry Ginnell, who accused the Government of committing murder. He also revealed that Lieutenant Burns, who was stationed at Fron-goch, had misused prisoners' money that was in his keeping.

Ginnell also visited Fron-goch, visits that R. M. Fox describes in *The Irish Citizen Army*:

His custom was to wear a frock coat with deep pockets behind the tails. When he appeared in the prison yard he was at once surrounded by a crowd of prisoners. While he exchanged greetings in loud tones he whispered, every now and then: 'Post office is open behind, lads; post office open behind!' This was a signal to dive into his back pockets in the crush, take out letters and smuggle others in. Ginnell was eventually forbidden entry for breaking prison regulations, but he outwitted the authorities at one time by giving his name in Irish. His wife, too, visited the prisoners and helped to get letters in and out.

A greater and greater number of MPs began to clamour for the men's release. On the 2nd of October the *Irish Independent* reported that through the Dublin Corporation, Alderman Alfie Byrne, MP had called for an amnesty for Irish prisoners who were being held without trial in English prisons and, pending such a move, for them to be treated as political prisoners. He demanded the formation of an All-Ireland Amnesty Association to pressurise the authorities into releasing them.

Byrne drew attention to the treatment of fifty-two internees at Fron-goch in particular. He read from a letter that had escaped the attention of the Censor, which complained about the punishment that was inflicted on those who refused to identify fellow prisoners. He also raised the Ash Pit Incident, the men's refusal to work in a nearby quarry, the poor standard of food, and an incident in which the internees were yoked to a lorry in order to drag shingle to North Camp.

Byrne read a report on the internees' living conditions which, he said, he had received from a private source. The report claimed that the men slept in badly ventilated and badly lit rooms, and got up in the morning in 'a semi-dazed and choking condition, and on the verge of collapse'. The report continued:

> Rats run riot in the dormitories day and night, and at night make themselves particularly unpleasant. Two water closets are provided inside each dormitory, and the stench from these adds considerably to the discomforts already mentioned.

The report also described the poor food, men fainting during the head-count or roll-call, the attempt to make them undertake quarry work and the punishment for refusing to identify fellow prisoners. It concludes that 'as a result of the treatment described above the men continuously suffer from neuralgia, toothache, colds, etc., and their health generally is seriously impaired'.

Byrne also mentioned the case of a man who had lost his reason as a result of the treatment. This was Daniel Devitt.

> He wandered in the fields, and for this he was given solitary confinement on bread and water. The man was a well educated, gentlemanly fellow who had lived on the North Circular Road.

Byrne concluded that the British authorities were treating the men at Fron-goch in a way that was worse than they alleged their own prisoners were treated by the Germans.

Another MP who won the respect of the men was William O'Brien from Mallow, who owned the *Cork Free Press*. Twice during October letters were sent to him outlining the conditions at Fron-goch. He made sure that these letters received widespread publicity. On the 11th of November, the publicity campaign reached its peak: under the headline 'The Shocking Story of Frongoch' the newspaper published details of the substandard food, the harsh living conditions and the strict regime the men were forced to endure there.

A statement was prepared in Fron-goch and circulated in Ireland which approved this story carried in the *Cork Free Press*. The statement emphasised that it was published not in the spirit of complaint but rather to show what existence was like in captivity with the English.

Following the pressure from the Dublin Corporation and in particular from Alfie Byrne, the camp authorities at last allowed a visit by an independent doctor, who was to be allowed to see for himself the living conditions endured by the men. Sir Charles Cameron, former Dublin City Council medical officer, was eighty-six years old. He was accompanied by Dr Braithwaite of the Home Office.

In an attempt to impress the visitors, the camp was cleaned, the internees were given new clothing, and new kitchen utensils were bought. Even the food was better, and butter replaced the usual margarine. However, when the two medical officers appeared the internees changed back into their old clothes and began to soil the walls and floors. Sixty men reported sick at the camp hospital.

During his visit, Cameron interviewed four internees, among them Michael Collins. When asked if there was anything in the camp that was not in short supply, Collins answered: 'Salt'. This trivial remark is the only reference to Collins made by W. J. Brennan-Whitmore in *With the Irish at Frongoch*.

Despite the anger of the camp authorities at the men's provocative behaviour, they improved the camp conditions, and Cameron, when Brennan-Whitmore later challenged him to deny that he had been harsh in his judgement on the condition of the camp, did not attempt to do so. This suggests that Cameron had indeed been critical of camp conditions.

It is quite possible that Cameron's visit and his ensuing response might have been at least partly responsible for the men's release a fortnight later, as was in part the death of Dr Peters, which was of sufficient concern to have been raised in Parliament. Indeed the whole question of the internees' situation was discussed at some length in Parliament. MP John Dillon raised the question of complaints made by internees that their letters were being held back. In reply, Home Secretary Sir George Cave promised an inquiry. It would be entrusted to the MP for Wigan, a Mr Neville.

The internees' situation had become a pressing concern in Parliament, and the question of their release grew apace. On Lloyd George's first day as Prime Minister he was pressed by John Redmond, who had by then taken the Sinn Féin position on internment, to release the men as a Christmas present for the people of Ireland. On the 21st of December this is exactly what Lloyd George did. The reason he gave, through his Home Secretary, was that the danger of keeping the men together was greater than the danger of releasing them.

The death of Dr Peters may not have directly led to Lloyd George's action but it might well have been a catalyst for the internees' release. The Prime Minister, renowned for his cunning, had perhaps understood that the remnants of that beaten, downcast rabble of Easter Week, soon to be the graduates of the Fron-goch University of Freedom, were now convinced revolutionaries.

7
Release

Freedom, when it came, was almost an anticlimax. Christmas was approaching, and the remaining men – almost six hundred of them – were resigned to spending it behind wire. They were, however, determined to enjoy it. The National Aid Committee in Ireland and in Britain, which had been set up to support the internees, had sent hampers of food. W. J. Brennan-Whitmore wrote of carloads of foodstuffs arriving at South Camp throughout Thursday and Friday prior to Christmas week. *The Daily Mail* announced:

> Ample supplies of geese, bacon, potatoes and sugar will be provided for the Irish prisoners in Frongoch Camp and Reading and Aylesbury Gaols during the Christmas season by the committee in Manchester, co-operating with the Dublin and London committees.

Though the men were resigned to spending Christmas in exile, they were stoical, according to Brennan-Whitmore. One internee told him that he would rather spend Christmas in Fron-goch than anywhere else – that is, if he was not sent home. Indeed, he believed that the men could do more good for Ireland in the camp than if they were released.

Release was at hand, however. Recording the events of the last week that he was to spend at Fron-goch (although he was not to know it at the time), M. J. O'Connor noted how cold the weather had become, 'King Frost being the reigning power'. On the 18th of December the time of the wake-up call had been put forward from 5.30 to 6.45 a.m. and the men received an extra blanket each. The long winter nights brought with them a sickness that was peculiar to the Camp. It was a depressing lethargy known by the men as 'that tired Frongoch feeling'.

The punishments continued. O'Connor described how one internee named M. Lynch, who was from County Cork and had been identified as being subject to conscription, refused to go to North Camp stating that he would have to be carried there. He was indeed carried there on a stretcher. Brennan-Whitmore refers to him as Miecal Lynch, and he was probably Michael F. Lynch from Ballyfeard. His brother Tim was also at the camp.

Pressure for the release of the men was mounting, as M. J. O'Connor notes:

> The British Government was in a bit of a 'stew'. They had over 500 Irishmen interned. These prisoners were held only on suspicion. No charge was, or very likely could be, preferred against them. The Government wished to get rid of the difficulty by letting them out, and having kept them now for $7\frac{1}{2}$ months without charge or trial they had to find some excuse for liberating them.

That excuse was provided by the arrival of Christmas. On the 22nd of December, O'Connor was not particularly surprised to read in an English paper a stop-press announcement of a statement made in the House of Commons the previous night by the Chief Secretary for Ireland, Henry Duke, that the men were to be allowed home with the least possible delay. O'Connor's account seems to contradict W. J. Brennan-Whitmore who recalled being told just after tea on the Friday evening, the 22nd, that the men were to be released. The order, he recalled, arrived from the Home Office by telegram. The men believed they would be kept till after Christmas because of the constraints of restricted train services combined with the holiday rush, but this was not to be the case. That night all those in North Camp were sent home on the eight o'clock train, and the following day those in the South Camp followed. It has been said that Lloyd George's primary reason for releasing the men had nothing to do with compassion. In the context of needing to draw the Americans into the war, he was more concerned about growing disquiet in the United States regarding the Irish situation. It seems therefore to be no coincidence that the men's release was announced on Lloyd George's first day as Prime Minister.

In preparation for their release, the internees were called to assemble by Lieutenant Burns, and were asked by him for the last time to acknowledge their names. This time it was for release purposes. The men, however, believed this to be another ploy to reveal the names of the refugees. Collins refused point blank. Burns declared that he had no further interest in finding Michael Murphy, or any other internee for that matter: the release was to be unconditional. Nevertheless, the men remained sceptical.

Burns explained that he was under orders to forward the names of all remaining internees to Dublin Castle, the headquarters of British administration in Ireland, and to the Home Office before the men could be released. After a discussion between Collins and Brennan-Whitmore, a compromise was reached: the men themselves would prepare a list of names. By Friday morning, the 22nd, that compromise was accepted and the release began.

The first batch to be released involved those from the north, south and west of Ireland. They were taken by special train to Holyhead, leaving Fron-goch, as one departing internee put it, to 'stew in its own isolation'. However, just as the men formed in lines on Fron-goch station platform, another problem arose. Burns, holding a travelling pass in his hand, called on Michael Flanagan and nineteen other internees who were travelling to Galway City to step forward. Suspecting a ploy even at the last minute, not one of the internees moved. On Brennan-

Whitmore's suggestion, Burns then rephrased the order and called for someone to step forward in Flanagan's name to receive the travel document. This was accepted.

On the Friday, the 22nd of December, a hundred and thirty men were released; they arrived at Kingston Harbour (Dún Laoghaire) the following morning. Those travelling on to the south and west left the train there while the remaining sixty-seven remained on board and left the train at Westland Row (now Pearse Street Station). From there they marched down Great Brunswick Street (Pearse Street) and Sackville Street (O'Connell Street). Some forty others reached Dublin on the cattle boat the *Slieve Bloom*, the very ship that had ferried them to captivity seven months previously. These men marched up the quay in military fashion, displaying their Sinn Féin badges.

On the Sunday, Christmas Eve, a hundred and thirty men reached Westland Row, while three hundred Dublin men arrived at North Wall on a steamer. Then, on Christmas morning, twenty-eight more men landed at Carlisle Pier and twenty went on to Dublin by rail. A total of six hundred and twenty-eight men, including some from Reading Gaol, were back on Irish soil.

Upon his arrival home at Clonakilty, Collins felt a sense of caution among the people. There he spent three weeks drinking 'Clonakilty wrastler on a Frongoch stomach' (wrastler being a kind of porter). Joe Sweeney, on the other hand, was welcomed back to Donegal by members of the Ancient Order of Hibernians and their band.

The Kerry men, fourteen of them, stopped off en route at an unidentified English railway station – probably Chester or Crewe. Here their leader Henry Spring ordered a round of beer. He was refused by the barmaid as the law forbade anyone to pay for alcoholic beverages for others. A policeman was called, but he failed to resolve the matter. The men were eventually ordered back on the train, but without paying for the drinks.

One batch of returning internees, while changing trains at Chester Station, began singing 'Deutschland, Deutschland über Alles'. No one took any notice. M. J. O'Connor described his journey home as being

> ... long and tedious, but the anticipation and delight of getting back once more after months of weary exile and at such a time as Christmas too, made up for all. The journey's end found anxious relatives and friends greeting weary and travel-stained home-comers. There were many happy homes and many festive boards made gay and merry during Christmas 1916 by the presence of occupants of places which had been long vacant in the family circle.

His account of the return from Fron-goch concludes optimistically:

> Amid the Christmas rejoicings I will draw this hastily compiled attempt at a record to a close and forget for a time such unwelcome and unhospitable spots as Prisons, Prison-Yards, Prison cells, plank beds, internment camps, Commandants, and last but not least that faraway hamlet in North Wales which contains Frongoch Camp, aptly named 'England's Purgatory'.

However, O'Connor was not allowed to forget for long. Two months later he was among twenty-eight arrested for their part in an alleged German invasion. Once more he was bound for Holyhead, on his way to Wetherby Gaol, where he would remain until July 1917.

Britain's obsession with the German connection reached its climax the following year. The German Plot was 'invented' by the British authorities at Dublin Castle, after the arrest of a man who was rescued from an island off the Galway coast during the spring of 1918. He explained that he had escaped from the wreck of an American ship. The fact that no such ship existed led the authorities to believe that his actions were suspect. The man, Joe Dowling, had been a member of Casement's Brigade. At his trial it was alleged that he had landed on the island off a German submarine. He was sentenced to penal servitude for life.

The discovery of Joe Dowling was all the excuse the authorities needed. On the night of the 17th of May, under Clause 14B of the Restoration of Order in Ireland Act, there were arrests throughout Ireland, and seventy-three people were taken to mainland Britain, including Arthur Griffith, Eamon de Valera, Count Plunkett and Countess Markievicz, as well as men who had done time at Fron-goch, including W. J. Brennan-Whitmore, Denis Mac Con Uladh (McCullough), Frank Drohan and M. J. O'Connor. The seventy-three who were arrested were taken to a disused army camp near Holyhead in north Wales for a week, before the group was split up and sent to Usk and Gloucester prisons. Some, including de Valera, were sent to Lincoln prison. Soon another twenty men followed them. It was alleged by the authorities that the German Plot went as far back as 1914, and that some of the activities were connected to a number of those who had been interned at Fron-goch. (Perhaps not coincidentally, most of those arrested had been elected to Parliament as Sinn Féin members.)

As soon as those accused were imprisoned, the struggle for prisoners' rights, which had begun at Fron-goch, continued – especially at Usk Prison in southeast Wales. The prison governor, Governor Young, soon caved in and agreed to the right of association, the right to write and receive letters and parcels, and the right for the prisoners to wear their own clothes. On the 21st of January 1919 four Irish prisoners managed to escape from Usk Prison using a rope ladder. Among them were Frank Shouldice and George Geraghty, two ex-Fron-goch internees. The plan had been for twenty men to escape, but a flu epidemic hindered them. Eleven days later, de

Valera escaped from Lincoln Jail, allegedly wearing a pair of plimsolls given him by ex-Fron-goch internee Tom Ruane.

The escapes, combined with the death of three prisoners from the effects of flu, embarrassed the Government and the prisoners were released. The first batch reached Ireland, led by Arthur Griffith, on the 19th of March 1919. It should be said that many influential people had harboured misgivings about the authenticity of the German Plot, none more so than Lord Wimborne, the recently deposed Lord Lieutenant of Ireland.

Just before Christmas 1916, however, the thought of being re-arrested was hardly envisaged. On their release from Fron-goch Séamas Ó Maoileoin and his returning companions were allowed to wander freely around Bala and mingle with the local people while they waited for their connecting train. The atmosphere surprised Ó Maoileoin:

> One would have thought that they would have been frightened to talk to us, frightened, perhaps, of the army. I noticed how loyal they were to their language. In all the shops, it was Welsh that they all spoke to each other even though we, the customers, could not understand one word. It is a totally different story in Ireland.

Many of the returning men carried with them baskets of food sent to them at Fron-goch for Christmas. At Liberty Hall in Dublin a celebration was organised for members of the ICA who had fought in the Rising, and the contents of many of the hampers were enjoyed there. The printing trays that had been used to carry type for the Proclamation were scrubbed and covered with paper and used as food trays. R. M. Fox describes the scene:

> And now the hampers are unpacked, the pink hams and the big plum puddings find their way to the table. Stories are told about the fighting in Easter Week at the different posts.

Old friends, reunited, call across from table to table; hands, used to hard toil, grip each other once more. Women tell of recent struggles in Dublin, of the offensive of all the dark forces after Easter Week, minimising their own efforts to keep homes together in the absence of the men.

The wild geese were home at last, their feathers ruffled but their wings unclipped.

8
From Bala to Béal na mBláth

The internees returned to an Ireland facing increasing conflict. Day by day, mounting British casualties in the Great War seemed to be bringing conscription in Ireland closer and Republicans nationwide were being arrested on trumped-up charges of having collaborated with Germany. The theoretical military strategies that had been taught at Fron-goch began to be put into practice. What started as isolated skirmishes turned into an all-out war that became known as the War of Independence, or later as the Tan War.

If Wales played a part in inspiring the Irish cause in Fron-goch, it also played a part in the oppression of the Irish movement towards independence. There were Welsh citizens among the Crown agents, some of whom were Welsh speakers. Lord Wimborne, Lord Lieutenant of Ireland, was a member of the Guest family from Glamorgan. He was surrounded by Welsh assistants. Dora Herbert Jones is named as one of Wimborne's agents in *Wrth Angor yn Nulyn* [At Anchor in Dublin] by Huw Llewelyn Williams. Later Dora Herbert Jones would become a great scholar in the field of Welsh folk music. In Ireland she attended Bethel Welsh Chapel in Talbot Street, along with with Selwyn Davies, a London Welshman who was Wimborne's secretary, and Beta Jones of Abercin near Cricieth, who was secretary to Lady Wimborne. Another devoted supporter of the same chapel was Ernest Blythe, a member of the Sinn Féin Executive who became Finance Minister in 1923.

It is likely that Lloyd George and Thomas Jones, his private secretary, were influential in recruiting these Welsh agents. It was Selwyn Davies who first introduced Dora Herbert Jones to Bethel Chapel, where she became the organist. In *Brenhines*

Powys [Queen of Powys] Gwenan Mair Gibbard describes Herbert Jones' role:

> By 1918 she was in Dublin and was involved in 'very secret' work at the Viceregal Lodge. She travelled regularly between Dublin and London for about eighteen months, at a time when travelling on the Packet from Holyhead could be very dangerous.

After graduating, Dora became the first woman to hold the post of secretary in the Commons, working for Sir Herbert Lewis, the MP for Flint. She married Welsh scholar Herbert Jones, who joined the Welsh Fusiliers and was badly injured at Ypres. She joined the Red Cross at Troyes at the behest of the Davies sisters who would later settle at Gregynog Mansion in mid Wales. While in Ireland she spent some time in Limerick, where her husband was recuperating. Following her return, she turned her attention to collecting and performing Welsh folk music and became full-time secretary to the Davies sisters and to their famous Gregynog Press.

Herbert Jones never seems to have discussed openly her 'very secret' work for Lord Wimborne, but the little Welsh chapel could well have been central to her plans. One regular visiting preacher was the Welsh pacifist George M. Ll. Davies, who is known to have been secretly used as an emissary between Lloyd George and de Valera. It is not clear if Ernest Blythe was involved in these comings and goings, or if, unbeknownst to the elders and the ordinary members, Bethel Chapel was being used for more worldly purposes. Perhaps Dora Herbert Jones, travelling so often between Dublin and Holyhead during her eighteen months at the Viceregal Lodge, was acting as a courier.

Huw Llewelyn Williams notes a bizarre incident connected with the Welsh Chapel. The family of Professor John

Lloyd-Jones, the Welsh poet and Professor of Welsh at University College, Dublin, employed a Catholic maid, and the Chapel House was also occupied by Catholics. When the maid's uncle died at Chapel House, she and her mother called round to put his affairs in order. While searching through his belongings they discovered some grenades and ammunition hidden in the chapel vestry. The arms were unceremoniously dumped in the Liffey.

Lord Wimborne was replaced in early summer 1919 by Lord French, who was known as the Earl of Ypres. Lord French took on the grand title of 'His Majesty's Lord-Lieutenant-General and General Governor of Ireland', and his appointment appears to have marked the end of Dora Herbert Jones' involvement in secret activities.

Wimborne was replaced several months into the War of Independence, which had begun on the 21st of January 1919. This was also the day that Dáil Éireann, the Irish Parliament, which was not recognised by Britain, held its first meeting. Also on the 21st, nine men, including those known as Collins' Big Four – Dan Breen, Seán Treacy, Seán Hogan and Fron-goch graduate Seamus Robinson – ambushed and stole a cart full of explosives at Soloheadbeg quarry in County Tipperary. Two policemen refused to surrender and reached for their weapons. Both were shot dead. Hogan was arrested but was rescued later, while he was being taken by train to Cork.

County Tipperary was immediately proclaimed a military area under the Defence of the Realm Act. On behalf of the Tipperary Brigade of the Volunteers, Robinson retaliated by proclaiming that anyone found in the South Riding area who supported the British Government would forfeit their lives. The Volunteer executive, however, countermanded this threat. The incident reflected the need for a united military policy among the Volunteers, and this would be the task of Richard Mulcahy in particular, along with Michael Collins.

The War of Independence served to unite Republicans, but that union was lost at the end of 1921 with the signing of the Treaty, which divided Ireland geographically as well as ideologically. Those who had been united and inspired by their experiences at Fron-goch found themselves on opposite sides of the fence.

During the War of Independence, however, Republicans were united in their opposition to the British Government and to the Government's Black and Tans and Auxiliaries groups. The organisation of the two Republican factions – the Irish Republican Brotherhood and the Volunteers – into the Irish Republican Army is difficult to date precisely. It does not appear to be the case that they evolved seamlessly from one to the other, but for some time they did exist more as one unit than as separate entities.

The Irish Republican Brotherhood emerged at the time of the Fenians as a secret movement whose members swore an oath of allegiance. This was by far the strongest faction in the Easter Rising, and Tom Clarke, one of the signatories of the Proclamation, wielded considerable power. The IRB was strengthened by association with Irish language movements, Gaelic clubs and Gaelic sports associations, especially the Gaelic Athletics Association. W. B. Yeats was a member, but some, such as W. J. Brennan-Whitmore, saw the IRB as a dangerously elite organisation.

The Volunteers, on the other hand, were formed in response to the arming of Ulster Protestants who were dedicated to destroying any measure of Home Rule. The formation of the Volunteers was a blessing for the IRB. It gave them cover to carry out their own activities with fewer restrictions.

It is far more difficult to find a date for the emergence of the Irish Republican Army. The name was used as early as the Easter Rising and many of the Fron-goch internees used the acronym 'IRA' after their names in the autograph books and albums in which they recorded their thoughts and memories of camp life. Among those who used it was John MacDonagh, brother of Thomas MacDonagh, a signatory of the Proclamation who had been executed. The Volunteers appear to have been gradually and inevitably taken over by the new title as they merged into one army.

It is believed that the IRA acronym was first used as far back as the Battle of Ridgeway in 1866 when Fenians in the USA planned to attempt an incursion into Canada. There the Fenian soldiers wore IRA insignia. Sean O Mahony believed that the definitive moment was when James Connolly proclaimed during the Easter Rising that henceforth there would be neither Irish Volunteers nor the Irish Citizen Army. There would be only one army, the Irish Republican Army. In a written order he also referred specifically to the IRA.

The name was used by Brennan-Whitmore in his book *With the Irish in Frongoch* which was published in 1917. In *Brother against Brother* Liam Deasy claims that the title IRA was adopted officially after a meeting of the Staff Headquarters in October 1919. Piaras Béaslaí, author of *With the IRA in the Fight for Freedom,* claimed that it was only gradually that the name became generally accepted. In December 1918 the Republican newspaper *An-tÓglach* [The Volunteer] stated that the Volunteers would in future be known as the Irish Republican Army.

The roots of today's IRA go back to the Treaty of 1921, when this Army was split between the Regulars and the Irregulars. The Regulars represented the official Irish Government and the Irregulars represented the Republicans who refused to accept the Treaty. The Irregulars were the forebears of the new IRA that followed, before another split at the end of the 1960s led to the formation of two groups: the Official and the Provisional IRA. During the ensuing years, there was further fragmentation, which led to the formation of the INLA (Irish National Liberation Army), and the IPLO (Irish People's Liberation Organisation) as well as other lesser-known movements. By the 1990s, there were more breakaway factions, including the Continuity IRA and the Real IRA. All the factions share one feature: they each profess to be the true inheritors of those who fought in the Easter Rising of 1916.

Those who participated in the Rising were placed together and described as Shinners, a derogatory reference to Sinn Féin, which was the political party formed by Arthur Griffith in 1905. After the Rising, Sinn Féin candidates swept the board, but the successful MPs refused to take their place in the British House of Commons. Countess Markievicz, a Sinn Féin member, was the first woman ever to be returned to the British Parliament.

When it was restructured in the spring of 1918, the Republican Army was still generally referred to as the Irish Volunteers. Dick McKee and Michael Collins began forming army divisions across the country. As Ulick O'Connor notes in *Michael Collins and The Troubles*, it was this organisation, and the military training that ensued, which led to the emergence of leaders such as Tom Barry of the 3rd West Cork Brigade, Liam Lynch in North Cork, the brothers Patrick and Michael Brennan in Clare (both of whom were Fron-goch graduates), Seán McKeon in Longford, Seán Moylan in Cork and Eoin O'Duffy in Monahan. These men became national folk heroes. Tom Barry, who became known as The General, was a major figure. When I met him in 1979, he was old, weak, deaf and almost blind but his handshake was as strong as that of a young man. Barry described the Flying Column, which used hit-and-run tactics, as 'the spearhead of the people's army'.

The arrival of the Tans and then the Auxiliaries in 1920 ensured that it would be known as the Year of Terror. Fewer and fewer native Irish people were prepared to risk recruitment to the Royal Irish Constabulary, the RIC, so the Tans were sent as reinforcements by Sir Neville Macready, Commander in Chief of Forces in Ireland. He had already earned a dubious reputation in Wales. It was Macready who, at Churchill's request, had sent in soldiers to ruthlessly quell the striking miners of Tonypandy in 1910.

The first contingent of Tans arrived at North Wall on the 25th of March 1920. They were paid ten shillings a day, but because of a shortage of uniforms they were kitted out in different shades of khaki, dark green and black, most of them wearing green or black caps and black leather RIC belts. The combination of black and khaki gave them their nickname, but there was also another source: a famous pack of foxhounds named the Black and Tans. By March 1921 there were seven thousand Tans in Ireland.

At the end of July 1920 the Tans were joined by the Auxiliary Cadets, or 'Auxies'. Recruited in London, these were ex-officers who had already proved themselves in battle. They were recruited as Temporary Cadets but held a rank equivalent to an RIC sergeant and were paid £1 per day plus allowances. The Auxies' uniform consisted of large tam-o'-shanter bonnets with the insignia of the crowned harp of the RIC; khaki tunics, breeches and puttees; a belt with bayonet and scabbard, and an open revolver holster on the right thigh. Later they wore a dark green Balmoral.

Both groups were allowed to act outside the law with absolute impunity. Sir Hamar Greenwood, who took over as Chief Secretary to Ireland, was instrumental in persuading Parliament to pass the Restoration of Order in Ireland Act, which gave the military and police virtually carte blanche powers. But as Collins observes in his *Notes*:

> This law in reality abolished all law in Ireland and left the lives and property of the people defenceless before the British forces.

Ordinary law was suspended, and internment on suspicion, secret trials, enter and search powers, confiscation without warrant, curfews, and the suppression of inquests were all permitted. Who would have believed that a British Labour Government would fight for much the same powers in 2005.

The Auxies were more feared than the Tans simply because they were more experienced and knowledgeable. Formed into companies of a hundred, they were sent as shock forces into IRA strongholds. Both the Auxies and the Tans, however, were ignorant of the guerrilla tactics that had been formulated and taught at Fron-goch and that were shortly to reach their full deployment, with Michael Collins playing a major part.

Curiously enough, W. J. Brennan-Whitmore, who was instrumental in teaching military tactics, only mentions Collins once by name in his account of camp life. This is strange, as both men knew each other well. Indeed, they had been together on the eve of the Rising. When I met Brennan-Whitmore in Dublin in July 1971 he was prepared to speak at length about his relationship with Collins, and about some of the leaders of the Rising.

Having lost both his parents when he was very young, he was brought up by an uncle and aunt in Ferns, County Wexford. He was proud of the fact that on his mother's side, the Brennans, he was a direct descendant of Father Murphy, one of the leaders of the 1798 rebellion. He explained:

> As far as I know, no one of any damned importance came from the Whitmore side of the family. I was often taunted regarding my double-barrelled surname. But I suffered in silence as my uncle and aunt, the last of the Whitmore branch, wanted the name to perpetuate.

Brennan-Whitmore became a shop assistant in Dublin and early in his life began writing. He sent a short story to Padraig

Pearse in the hope of seeing it published. The story was returned with a few words of encouragement. Pearse suggested that he needed more experience, but Brennan-Whitmore felt that he was already as good a writer as Dickens, and Pearse's criticism hurt him. In the depth of his disappointment and anger he was wandering in Dublin that night and, seeing a recruiting poster, joined the Irish Brigade in India, where he became an officer.

He knew nothing much about Irish history until he was recovering from an injury in an Indian hospital. A Catholic priest serving there introduced him to the works of nationalists such as Fintan Lawler and Arthur Griffith. Dismissed from the army on medical grounds he returned to work on his uncle's farm at Ferns and joined Sinn Féin and the Gaelic League.

After attending a recruiting meeting for the Irish Volunteers in Dublin in 1913, Brennan-Whitmore was visited by four men who asked him to form a local Volunteer Company. At first he refused, because he believed that facing Britain in an armed struggle would be futile. Father Michael Murphy, a local priest, managed to change his mind. Brennan-Whitmore was adamant, however, that as soon as he had trained the local men adequately, he would not participate further.

Shortly afterwards, he met a man who would play an important part in his life: J. J. O'Connell. O'Connell had been sent by Sean MacDiarmada as a liaison officer. Brennan-Whitmore remembered:

My main reluctance in getting involved was the fear that any loss of life among the young recruits would be blamed on me. Then Eamonn Ceannt challenged me to write a handbook on guerrilla tactics. I took up his challenge and wrote the book and it became the blueprint for the Volunteers.

By 1916, Brennan-Whitmore was Senior Staff Officer of the Volunteers and on Shrove Tuesday he was called to liaison with Thomas MacDonagh in Dublin. As he boarded the train he spotted two police officers trailing him. Just before the train reached Dublin he jumped off and continued his journey by tram. After having booked in to the Royal Exchange hotel in Parliament Street he sent a warning to MacDonagh. When he was stopped by the police he adopted an English accent and was allowed to proceed.

With MacDonagh he visited a Volunteer headquarters at Great Brunswick Street, where he met de Valera for the first time. 'I disliked him from the moment I saw him, and I still despise him,' he said to me in the interview.

On the following morning he left for Liberty Hall hoping to return to his hotel for lunch, but he was not to see the Royal Exchange for eight months. At Liberty Hall his first order was to move Joseph Plunkett from hospital, where he was dying of tuberculosis. There to assist him was Michael Collins, and Brennan-Whitmore described how Collins picked Plunkett up in his arms as if he were carrying a baby.

Upstairs in Liberty Hall, with Plunkett as well as Connolly and Pearse, he spotted a sheaf of posters bearing the headline 'Poblacht na hEirann' [The Irish Republic]. He described his terror when he read the words: 'Having organised her manhood through her secret revolutionary organisation, the Irish Republican Brotherhood … ' He knew then that the men who had visited him earlier in Wexford to try and recruit him were Irish Republican Brotherhood agents:

Had I learnt of this only a fortnight sooner, no one would have seen hide or hair of me in Dublin. In every address to my men I had emphasised that we would win because we were an open organisation. But by now it was too late to turn back. Connolly's small Irish Citizen Army was already lined up outside. Connolly himself issued the order and off they went followed by horse-drawn wagons.

On that first day of the Rising, Brennan-Whitmore found himself helping to fortify the building, before he was summoned by Connolly to take ten men to secure the building across the street. They were armed with sticks and a few guns. They barricaded the entrance to Talbot Street with furniture commandeered from nearby shops and houses. But no sooner had an armchair been thrown out of one house than the irate owner, an old woman, tried to retrieve it. Brennan-Whitmore had to threaten her at gunpoint before she reluctantly left for the relative safety of her home.

The next tactic was to break through the walls of the adjoining houses, which cleared a way through the street from end to end. On the Tuesday morning Brennan-Whitmore was informed by Pearse that the Volunteers in Wexford had risen up. On the Wednesday his complement of men rose to around forty. Then the looting and shelling began, forcing Brennan-Whitmore and his men to retreat. They had formulated a plan which would involve getting round the back of the British troops and hitting them from behind, but by then the city centre was surrounded and they were forced to surrender. Fortunately for Brennan-Whitmore, he had discarded his officer's uniform, so he was regarded as being just an ordinary Volunteer. 'That is why I was moved from Knutsford to enjoy the freedom of Fron-goch,' he said.

Like many of his contemporaries, Brennan-Whitmore remembered Collins at Fron-goch as a man who could not contemplate losing, even at play, and as a man who would not think twice of cheating in order to achieve his aims. When Brennan-Whitmore presented his series of lectures at Fron-goch which were based on his handbook on guerrilla tactics, Collins, not being among the leaders, was not allowed to attend, but Brennan-Whitmore relented and decided to allow him to be present. He remarked:

Today I would like to believe that he learnt something from those lectures. Whatever sad consequences the Treaty brought about, no one can deny Collins his greatness and his humanity.

The first thing Brennan-Whitmore did after his release from Fron-goch was to settle his hotel bill at the Royal Exchange. He was invited by his fellow ex-internee William Sears, editor of the *Enniscorthy Echo*, to join his journalistic staff. He remained Consultant Staff Officer of the Volunteers and described himself as the 'last surviving Commandant from 1916'. He was the last editor of *An t'Oglach*.

Many of Michael Collins' contemporaries at Fron-goch remembered him more as a noisy braggart than as a tactical planner and soldier, and later politician. It may well be that this image of the wrestling, pillow-fighting rebel was deliberately cultivated by Collins as a disguise that the future leader could hide behind. He would adopt similar tactics while on the run, playing the part of the hail-fellow-well-met.

It was at Fron-goch that he was nicknamed the Big Fellow, which, according to Frank O'Connor, reflected contempt rather than respect:

His companions summed up the side of him they most disliked in one scornful phrase – the Big Fellow! 'Collins thinks he's a big fellow,' they repeated. The nickname stuck; henceforth he was the Big Fellow, and the story of his brief life is the story of how he turned the scornful nickname into one of awe and affection.

The involvement of Collins in Fron-goch is so intertwined with the history of the Irish Republic that what happened to him after he left the camp and what happened to Ireland after his death are all interconnected. Indeed, Wales can claim to have played a part in his formative years, as the two men who most influenced Collins were both of Welsh descent. Thomas Davis (1814 – 1845) was the founder of Young Ireland and composed 'A Nation Once Again' and 'The West's Awake'. His father was Welsh and served in the Royal Artillery as a surgeon. Davis, a Protestant, was proud of his Welshness but stated that his family had lived for so long in England that they were regarded as being English.

Even more important than Davis to Collins was Arthur Griffith, the founder of Sinn Féin, who wrote a series of articles in the *United Irishman* that captured Collins' imagination. Griffith confirmed his Welsh roots to D. J. Williams, when they met in Dublin in 1920. Griffith's family roots were in the Caernarfon area.

During the Rising, Collins was the youngest Volunteer officer. Following his capture he was taken to Stafford Gaol, before he was transferred to Fron-goch. He may have spent the first three weeks of liberation from Fron-goch in drinking, but he was very soon back in the thick of things organising military training, smuggling arms, arranging loans and, most importantly, selecting his own secret squad named the Twelve Apostles to counteract the growing threat of British Intelligence. The idea of this execution squad was spawned at Fron-goch. The names of the Big Four, already mentioned, were well known to the authorities. These were Collins' chief soldiers in the field and as such had a heavy price on their heads. Of the four, only Seán Treacy was to lose his life during the fighting. Seamus Robinson, who was trained at Fron-goch, went on to oppose the Treaty.

Because the faces of the Big Four were well known, Collins needed a secret network of spies and assassins to strike back at and execute British Intelligence agents. As leader of the squad he chose Mick McDonnell, who had been a cook in Fron-goch's North Camp. He was later replaced as leader by yet another Fron-goch man, Paddy Daly. At the camp, Daly had been a continual irritant to the authorities. He instigated a hunger strike when he was refused permission to write home to his wife and was subsequently jailed for fifty-six days with hard labour at Walton Prison in Liverpool. Martin Savage was another Fron-goch graduate. He was killed during an unsuccessful ambush of Lord French (one of several such attempts) on the 19th of December 1919. He was commemorated in a song written by Wolf Stephens and popularised by Dominic Behan.

Two other ex-Fron-goch internees to join the Apostles were Jim Slattery and Tom Ennis, but the most famous ex-Fron-goch man among the Apostles was Bill Stapleton, who adopted the name George Moreland because, as he explained to Ulick O'Connor, he thought it sounded both Protestant and Jewish. The Squad's original meeting place was the Antient Concert Hall in Brunswick Street, but they moved to bigger premises in an old shop in Abbey Street, where they took on the role of house-painters, dressing accordingly in overalls and taking genuine orders from customers. When a call came that a spy sent over to assassinate Collins had been spotted, or that a member of the Igoe Gang was to be executed, two or three of the Apostles would leave the shop and, at a given sign from one of Collins' intelligence agents, would carry out the execution.

Stapleton reported to O'Connor that it would sometimes take all day to find the target. On other occasions, the members of the Squad would have detailed orders and the target would be identified by one of Collins' spies from Dublin Castle. He claimed that great care was taken when ordering an execution and in identifying the subject, so that innocent people would not be killed, but as he remarked to O'Connor, the members of the Squad considered themselves to be soldiers doing their duty. Following an execution he would often go to church to pray for the soul of the man he had just killed.

Such executions were portrayed in the press as cowardly

acts. Bill Stapleton and Joe Dolan once ordered a passenger off a No. 8 tram in Landsdowne Road and shot him. He was a well-known magistrate named Alan Bell, but, according to Richard Mulcahy, he was also an intelligence man who had obtained details of the Sinn Féin bank account, and his information could have jeopardised the future of the Republican movement. It seemed that Bell had also been working as a police spy since the 1880s in the west of Ireland. Piaras Béaslaí considers Bell to be the most important member of British Intelligence in Ireland.

Collins' campaign against enemy agents began to hit home. He soon had a bounty of £10,000 on his head. The pro-British press made a concerted effort to portray Collins as a fanatic who murdered for the sake of murder. Ironically the popular image of him as a gunman is misplaced: apart from his time in the Rising, he rarely carried a gun until his later days.

The press proclaimed to Collins that no matter how many agents were assassinated, others would fill their shoes. Collins' reply to this was to concede that England could always find someone to fill a dead agent's shoes, but no one could be found to step inside a dead agent's mind and acquire his information. Tim Pat Coogan claims that Collins developed a tactic of capturing enemy information rather than bricks and mortar. It was such inside knowledge that allowed Collins to move early on Sunday the 21st of November and strike at the very heart of British intelligence, in what became known world-wide as Bloody Sunday.

It says a lot for Collins' brilliance at organisation that only one Volunteer was arrested for being directly involved in the Bloody Sunday assassinations. This was Frank Teeling who was on lookout when he was captured and sentenced to death, but this did not stop the authorities from making other arrests in connection with the assassinations. Ex-Fron-goch internee Patrick Moran was also sentenced to death, although he had a cast-iron alibi. His confidence that he would not be hanged was so strong that he spurned the chance to escape from Kilmainham Gaol.

The escape was initiated by Collins through Ernie O'Malley, Officer Commanding of the 2nd Southern Division. Arrested under an assumed name, O'Malley gained the confidence of two privates in the Welsh Guards who were acting as prison warders. The two Welshmen, Ernest Roper and J. Holland, smuggled a gun and a bolt-cutter to O'Malley's cell. Together with Frank Teeling and Simon Donnelly, who took Patrick Moran's place, they managed to escape on the 21st of February 1921 after an earlier aborted attempt.

Simon Donnelly, like Moran, was an ex-Fron-goch internee, but while Donnelly got away, Moran stayed behind and was hanged. His confidence that justice would prevail had been sadly misplaced. The two Welsh Guards conspirators were both sentenced to eight years' hard labour.

Patrick Moran was one of six Volunteers hanged on the 14th of March 1921. He and Thomas Bryan, one of the six who was hanged, had both been at Fron-goch. Bryan was an electrician who was arrested during an attack on a British Army vehicle at Drumcondra. The others hanged that day were Frank Flood, Bernard Ryan, Patrick Doyle and Thomas Whelan.

Between November 1920 and June 1921 no less than twenty-four Volunteers were hanged. One of these, hanged on the 26th of April 1921, was another ex-Fron-goch man, Tom Traynor, who was the camp cobbler, and father of ten children. He had fought side by side with de Valera in the Rising. A prominent member of the Dublin Brigade, he was arrested following the killing of two soldiers in Brunswick Street (Pearse Street).

As the killings continued, however, secret negotiations were proceeding that eventually led to a truce. On the 12th of July, de Valera, Austin Stack, Arthur Griffith, Robert Barton, Count Plunkett and Erskine Childers crossed together to London. Two days later both sides met and the Prime Minister spent some time talking of Celtic matters, including the two native languages of Wales and Ireland.

The truce came and went, but discussions continued. Soon another delegation was back in London; this time it included Collins, but not de Valera. Collins' part in the negotiations that led to the Treaty will be discussed and argued for a long time to come. What ensued was the Civil War, in which the centre of Dublin, for the second time in five years, went up in flames. During the Civil War, ex-Fron-goch internees became enemies: the pro-Treaty Regulars of the Free State Army, and the anti-Treaty Irregulars of the Irish Republican Army.

Despite the debacle of the Rising, the lessons that had been taught at Fron-goch were not remembered: the Four Courts and other symbolic rather than strategic buildings were taken by the Irregulars, who reverted to static tactics.

Fron-goch ex-internees featured prominently in the events played out at the Four Courts. The attack on the Irregulars was led by Tom Ennis, who had been Commandant of the 2nd Dublin Brigade. In the Free State Army he reached the rank of Major General and was regarded by friend and foe as a fine soldier.

In June, Leo Henderson had been arrested by Government forces for commandeering military vehicles. The Irregulars hit back by kidnapping J. J. 'Ginger' O'Connell, the Government's Deputy Chief of Staff. To all accounts and purposes it was this incident that ignited the Civil War. Henderson and O'Connell had both been comrades at Fron-goch, the latter having served as Commandant of the South Camp.

The Civil War became bloodier and bloodier. By September 1922 some five thousand Republicans had been imprisoned without charge. During the Tan War, two dozen Republicans had been executed by the British. During the Civil War, seventy-seven Republicans – later revised to seventy-eight – were officially executed by their erstwhile comrades. In all it is estimated that the Civil War accounted for seven hundred and fifty pro-Treaty deaths. There are no official figures for Republican deaths during the same period, but they were considerably higher. The cost of the damage caused was estimated at around £50 million.

Between June 1920 and 1922, four hundred and twenty-eight people were killed in the North and some two hundred and thirty thousand Catholics driven from their homes.

Despite the success of the guerrilla warfare that had been theorised at Fron-goch and practised during the Tan War, it was not until August 1922 that Liam Lynch, Chief of Staff of the Republican Army, reverted to guerrilla tactics. He had little choice, as by then not one square foot of Irish soil remained under Republican control.

To Republicans, the Free State merely continued the dirty work that had been started by the British. Collins, however, was unrepentant. In notes he made in August 1922 he accused the Republicans of directing their fight not only against the national government and the national army but, worst of all, also against the Irish people:

> The anti-national character of their campaign became clear when we saw them pursuing exactly the same course as the English Black and Tans.... But the Black and Tans, with all their foreign brutality, were unable to make Ireland 'an appropriate hell'. The Irregulars brought their country to the brink of a real hell.

Collins noted that, having got rid of the British, the future mission of the Free State was to get rid of British influence – to de-Anglicise Irish people. At the back of his mind would have been the memories of the Welsh farmers and tradesmen whom he had met at Fron-goch and who, despite everything, had managed to keep their language and culture alive. He stressed that 'not a single British soldier, nor a single British official, will ever step again upon our shores, except as guests of a free people'.

Meanwhile, the executions continued. Even as late as 1940, Fron-goch veteran Patrick McGrath was executed together with Thomas Harte. The Justice Minister who signed their death warrant was Gerry Boland, who had been with McGrath at Fron-goch.

Collins died as he had lived – ever impetuous, ever defiant. Controversy still surrounds the circumstances of his death but its effect was widespread. Tom Barry was in Kilmainham Prison when the news reached the Republican prisoners who were being held there. He remembered the silence that descended over the prison, followed by a progressive whispering from the cells below. When he looked down he saw an astonishing sight: about a thousand Republican prisoners had begun an impromptu recitation of the rosary, a prayer for the peaceful repose of the soul of their former enemy, Michael Collins. By now he had undoubtedly earned the right to be recognised as the Big Fellow in the true sense of the description: the contempt of that nickname given to him at Fron-goch had indeed changed to respect.

Back in those Fron-goch days, one of his closest comrades had been Seán Hales. Two of Hales' brothers were interned there as well, while another brother, Tom, had managed to escape. All four had been prominent during the Tan War. Tom Hales was captured but despite undergoing torture, refused to reveal the whereabouts of Collins. When Collins was killed in Béal na mBláth on the 21st of August 1922, Tom Hales was among the half-dozen who ambushed him. When he heard who had been killed, he broke down and wept.

As the Free State Government strengthened its hold, it not only reaffirmed the legitimacy of the Defence of the Realm Act, which had been used so ruthlessly by the British against the Irish, but it also adopted more stringent powers. Richard Mulcahy, the Defence Minister, submitted proposals for an Emergency Powers Bill which effectively allowed reprisal executions. Under its provisions, any Act of War by the Republicans carried the death penalty, which was to be handed down at Military Tribunals. Under the Bill, Acts of War could range from being found in possession of arms to looting or destroying property. The Cabinet endorsed the Bill, and it was even supported by a pastoral issued by the Catholic Church. Mulcahy as Defence Minister and Sean MacMahon as Commanding Officer of the Free State Army now held limitless powers of arrest. They could arrest and imprison anyone without enquiry, accusation or trial. The military courts were held in secret and no Republican soldiers had the right to be treated as a prisoner of war. Since the days of Fron-goch the wheel had turned full circle: MacMahon and Mulcahy were both ex-Fron-goch internees, as were many who were responsible for the executions and killings that followed.

9
Two Lord Mayors

Terence MacSwiney and Tomás MacCurtain will be forever inextricably linked in life and in death. Having joined the Volunteers at the same time in 1913, having served time together at Fron-goch and Reading, and having been released together, the two Lord Mayors of Cork City died within seven months of each other in 1920.

There the similarity ends. Tomás MacCurtain died quickly and brutally, shot at his home by a murder gang made up of disguised members of the Royal Irish Constabulary. Terence MacSwiney died an excruciating and lingering death following a ten-week prison hunger strike.

Despite the fact that neither of them took part in the Rising, they were both arrested and interned at Fron-goch. The confusion and miscommunication that had prevailed over the Easter period resulted in only a handful of men taking up arms in Cork – notably the Kent family from Fermoy. As they were arrested, one policeman and one of the three Kent brothers, Richard, were shot dead.

There were others like the Kents who were eager to fight. Among these were members of the Hales and the O'Donoghue families of Ballinadee. Although MacCurtain and MacSwiney had set up headquarters in Cork City on Easter Monday, they ultimately managed to persuade the others that the Rising was off. At the time MacCurtain was the leader of the Irish Republican Brotherhood in the area, and was responsible for informing the Limerick Volunteers of the decision to call off the Rising, while MacSwiney was his deputy, and was responsible for passing on Eoin MacNéill's countermanding order in Kerry. MacNéill had originally called for the Rising to begin on

Easter Sunday only to cancel it because of the lack of organisation. Those countermanding orders had been brought to Cork by J. J. 'Ginger' O'Connell, who himself would be sent to Fron-goch – indeed, he was the first Volunteer Officer Commanding to be interned there.

So determined were the Hales brothers to fight, that MacSwiney had to visit them personally in order to persuade them to accept MacNéill's order not to take action. By the time Pearse's call to ignore that order and to indeed arm had arrived, it was too late. Cork City was by then surrounded by British troops and Volunteer movement was impossible. Despite not taking part, three of the Hales brothers and three of the O'Donoghues were arrested, together with MacSwiney, on the 3rd of May, nine days after the Rising began on the 24th of April. The authorities had broken their promise that no further action would be taken if the Volunteers surrendered their arms. All but one of the Hales brothers were interned at Fron-goch.

MacCurtain was arrested a week after the Rising, and on the 22nd of May both future Lord Mayors were sent with a hundred and thirty-nine other Volunteers from Cork Gaol to Richmond Barracks in Dublin. The men were handcuffed in pairs for the journey. Unlike the reception experienced by the majority of internees when they were escorted along Dublin streets to the awaiting cattle boat, MacCurtain and his comrades, according to his own testimony, were warmly acclaimed by the watching crowds when they made the journey on the 30th of May. By then, of course, fifteen leaders had been shot, and the Volunteers had become heroes. Both men were sent to Wakefield Prison on the 1st of June and ten days later they arrived together at Fron-goch.

Upon their arrival they were elected members of the Executive Committee of the General Council. MacCurtain was also chosen to oversee the Gaelic classes. Both MacCurtain and MacSwiney were influential in the move to transform the

General Council from an administrative organisation into a military body. Under the new order, MacCurtain was put in charge of Dormitory 2 and MacSwiney was put in charge of Dormitory 4, both in the South Camp.

In *Enduring the Most: the Life and Times of Terence MacSwiney* Francis J. Costello relates a strange incident when MacSwiney clashed with Gearóid O'Sullivan, an Irish Republican Brotherhood member, over the refusal on the part of some of the men to clean out latrines and slop-buckets for the guards. MacSwiney believed that they should obey reasonable orders, but O'Sullivan prevailed. Costello also notes that MacSwiney was once placed in solitary confinement, but does not specify the offence.

Seán T. O'Kelly reveals how adept MacSwiney was at bribing camp officials. He managed to persuade one official to let the men read their mail prior to it being censored:

> It was MacSwiney himself who used to give out the letters every day. We used to read them in half an hour. Then they would be back in the hands of the censor and ready for sending to the censor of Post in London.

For this service, the officials received bribes of two bottles of beer a day. After those same letters had been scrutinised in London, they would be returned heavily censored, sometimes with entire pages missing.

On the 27th of June MacSwiney was visited at Fron-goch by his sister Mary. They met at 2.00 p.m. and were given only a quarter of an hour together. Mary took the opportunity to visit MacCurtain as well. She applied for another meeting with her brother but was refused. Two MPs backed her application, J. C. Dowdall and Tim Healy. Indeed, Healy raised the matter in Parliament on the 6th of July and was told by the Home Secretary that it would not be possible, as Fron-goch was 'overwhelmed with visitors'.

Mary MacSwiney worked tirelessly for the Republican internees at Fron-goch and in various English prisons. In Liverpool she organised a support committee that arranged to send to Fron-goch a portable altar, a harmonium, washing utensils, soap, clothes and a football. She also succeeded in enlisting the support of Father Thomas McGarvey, who was a tireless worker in the campaign for prisoners' rights.

It seems that MacSwiney was not at peace with himself at Fron-goch. A prisoner called Sheehan wrote to Mary, describing her brother as being in good spirits but 'a little grave and probably chafing at confinement. I think he is suffering a bit from the heat or nerves'.

The soldier in MacSwiney, however, was still active. According to J. J. O'Connell, who was with him at Fron-goch and later at Reading, MacSwiney was 'the main inspiration in insisting on the continuation of theoretical military study'. At MacSwiney's instigation, the internees were given instruction in military drill both in Fron-goch and in Reading, as well as instructions in signalling, history, and analysis of the fighting techniques then current in the Great War.

It was on the 11th of July that MacSwiney and MacCurtain were removed from Fron-goch and sent to Reading Gaol, where those who were thought to be the hard core of the Volunteers were imprisoned. The MacCurtain Papers include letters of goodbye from some of MacCurtain's Fron-goch colleagues. Paul Dawson Cusack, a County Longford man and a member of the camp's Amusements Committee wrote:

> I find it difficult to say good-bye. We have talked so much, laughed so much and got so well acquainted that I am afraid that if I were to say all I feel, you would consider it exaggerated.

Thomas Boylan, a Dubliner who was a member of the General Council and a teacher at Fron-goch wrote:

> Not being a man of many words I cannot say all that I should wish to say to you but from my heart of hearts I wish you God Speed. My constant prayer shall be for you that you be imbued with fortitude and to bear well and bravely whatever may be inflicted on you, and that soon you will be restored to friends and liberty.

Both men were freed from Reading Gaol on Christmas Eve 1916, and they immediately threw themselves into the work of recruiting members and procuring arms. According to Francis J. Costello, Fred Murray (himself a Volunteer) stated that MacSwiney 'felt keenly the failure of the Rising in Cork and the false position he was placed in through it'.

Most historians agree that MacSwiney and MacCurtain were still smarting from the consequences of their mistaken and successful attempt to stop the Rising in Cork. At Fron-goch some Cork internees were often reminded by others – especially by Dubliners – of their failure to take up arms. Cork was one of the most rebellious areas in Ireland, especially West Cork. In *The IRA and its Enemies* Peter Hart claims that 'the keenest Cork graduates of Frongoch and Richmond came from the Bandon and Macroom Battalions and the Cobh Company. Men like the Haleses, Begleys, Mannings and Walshes...'

Despite – and probably because – of the military failure of the Easter Rising, both MacCurtain and MacSwiney together with another Fron-goch veteran, Michael Brennan of West Clare, enthusiastically canvassed for a second Rising early in 1919. The idea they proposed was to attack police barracks in a particular area and then move on and do exactly the same in another area. The leaders in Dublin rejected these notions and Richard Mulcahy in particular viewed such a move as a mobile insurrection and the whole idea was shelved.

This was more of a difference of opinion than a split. Mulcahy had been best man at MacSwiney's wedding. He was in open detention in Bromyard when he married Muriel Murphy on the 8th of June 1917. They were married at Bromyard Catholic Chapel, and MacSwiney wore full Volunteer regalia.

Meanwhile, following the electoral victory for Sinn Féin by Count Plunkett in the Roscommon by-election on the 3rd of February 1917, the authorities arrested twenty-six leaders of various national organisations (twenty-eight, according to M. J. O'Connor) including MacCurtain, MacSwiney and Seán T. O'Kelly, and charged many of them under DORA, the Defence of the Realm Act. Transgressions included exhibiting the tricolour, uttering statements that could cause discontent, and singing disloyal songs. Despite such harassment tactics, Joseph McGuinness was elected on the 9th of May as Sinn Féin TD for South Longford.

On the 30th of January 1920, soon after being elected as Councillor for Cork North West, MacCurtain was elected Lord Mayor of Cork. From the beginning he set about eradicating corruption in local government, and from the outset received threats. He had been carefully observed by the Royal Irish Constabulary for some years. Many prominent Republicans received death threats written on official Dáil Éireann [Irish Parliament] notepaper that had been stolen by the Royal Irish Constabulary during a raid. This made it appear that the Republicans were split.

By 1920, County Cork was a ferment of rebelliousness: a third of the British Army in Ireland was located there. It was there that the British policy of reprisal killings reached its lowest depths. In *The IRA at War 1916-1923* Peter Hart describes the Bandon area as 'the Gaza strip of the Irish *intifada*'. According to Hart, that one area produced eleven times as many casualties as the whole of County Antrim.

In *The Black and Tans* Richard Bennett claims that Lloyd George entirely supported the idea of reprisal killings, and the premise that two Republicans should be killed for every loyalist death. In West Cork in particular the Black and Tans and the Auxiliaries ran riot, killing and looting on a whim, but their acts were often reprisals for the mounting success of the hit-and-run tactics used by the Volunteers' Flying Columns, such as Tom Barry's fabled 3rd West Cork Brigade.

MacCurtain was Commandant of the 1st Cork Brigade, and he was the victim of such a reprisal in 1920. During the early hours of that 20th of March, a gang of armed men began smashing down the door of the MacCurtain family home on Thomas Davis Street. Tomás' wife Elizabeth opened the door and they rushed in. The men were in disguise. According to evidence she provided, one had 'a black face and eyes shining like a demon'. Some of them spoke with English accents. One of them held Elizabeth while two others ran upstairs and as MacCurtain came out of his bedroom to investigate, he was shot twice before his terrified family. He died minutes later. It was his thirty-sixth birthday.

MacCurtain's death had a profound effect on Michael Collins. In a letter to MacSwiney he wrote: 'I have not very much heart in what I am doing today thinking of poor Tomás. It is surely the most appalling thing that has been done yet'.

The authorities tried to blame discontented Republicans for MacCurtain's death. The inquest, however, returned a clear and unambiguous verdict:

> We find that Alderman Tomás MacCurtain, Lord Mayor of Cork, died from shock and haemorrhage, caused by bullet wounds, and that he was wilfully wounded under circumstances of the most callous brutality: and that the murder was organised and carried out by the RIC officially

directed by the British Government.

We return a verdict of wilful murder against David Lloyd George, Prime Minister of England; Lord French, Lord Lieutenant of Ireland; Ian MacPherson, late Chief Secretary of Ireland; Acting Inspector General Smith of the RIC, Divisional Inspector Clayton of the RIC; DI Swanzy and some unknown members of the RIC.

In *Raids and Rallies*, Ernie O'Malley blames MacCurtain's death on the Igoe Gang, the first murder gang to operate secretly in Ireland. It was named after their leader, Eugene Igoe, a Royal Irish Constabulary Sergeant, and according to O'Malley its members came from the Dovea and Thurles area. Their policy was to target particular Republicans. If their targets did not happen to be at home then their brothers would do. It was generally assumed that such men operated with the blessing of the authorities, or that at least the authorities were more than willing to look the other way. MacCurtain had long been targeted and had been warned by his old friend from Fron-goch days, Micháel Ó Cuill. MacCurtain chose to ignore every warning.

Oswald R. Swanzy, regarded as the man who was directly responsible for the killing (although Peter Hart maintaines that there was a doubt regarding his guilt), was sent for his own safety to Lisburn in the loyalist stronghold of County Antrim. When the 1st Cork Brigade heard of this, there was much debate as to who would be given the task – indeed the honour – of avenging their Commandant's murder. However, because the Cork accent would stand out in the north, Collins decided to send just one man: the Brigade's Intelligence Officer, Seán Culhane, who knew Swanzy. Some maintain that Dick Murphy was also present. Culhane was given MacCurtain's own pistol to carry out the job, which was typical of Collins' style of vengeance.

Culhane went north and met up with a small party of Belfast Volunteers. It was Sunday the 22nd of August and Culhane recognised his target among a crowd of worshipers leaving church. He shouted Swanzy's name. The District Inspector made the fatal mistake of responding, which allayed any doubts about his identity. Culhane shot him with the words, 'Take that for MacCurtain!'

The inevitable reprisals came. British troops, police and members of the Ulster Volunteer Force rioted for twenty-four hours, killing one citizen, burning and looting some sixty buildings, and making scores of Catholics homeless.

Swanzy's killing did little to change the British Government policy of assassinating prominent Republican citizens. In Limerick the following year the Mayor, George Clancy, and his predecessor, Michael O'Calaghan, were both shot dead on the 7th of March. There had been a plot to kill the Right Reverend Dr Michael Fogarty, the Bishop of Killaloe, who was a Republican sympathiser, but that particular conspiracy failed.

MacCurtain was succeeded by MacSwiney as Commandant of the 1st Cork Brigade and as Lord Mayor of Cork. MacSwiney was also elected to the First Dáil (Irish Parliament) for Mid Cork, but he still found time to write, to travel and to lecture on independence. To him the Irish language was synonymous with independence, and he demanded that others should correspond with him in Irish. In a speech in Kilkenny he said: 'Our language is the boundary wall between Ireland and England; Irish freedom cannot be permanent … unless we succeed in saving Irish from extinction'.

On the 21st of August 1920 the British Government announced the Restoration of Order Act in Ireland. The act provided relief for military forces in Ireland from almost all restraints of law. In effect it meant that four-fifths of the population, those who had voted for an Irish Parliament, were offenders. Any Irish citizen could be jailed without charge or trial for an indefinite period.

One of the first to be held under the new Act was MacSwiney. He was arrested with twenty-one Volunteer leaders at a meeting at City Hall on the 12th of August. He was the only leader of note in the eyes of the authorities. At Cork Gaol he and eleven others immediately began a hunger strike. On the third day of his detention, MacSwiney was sent in a warship to south Wales – probably Swansea – and on by train to London and to Brixton Prison. He was charged with having in his possession two secret documents, described as police cipher codes, and with being in possession of notes for a speech calling for an uncompromising war against Britain. He was found guilty and sentenced to two years in prison. In his speech from the dock he vowed to continue his hunger strike and – alive or dead – he would be released a free man. In other words, he would emerge a free man or be freed by death. In all, MacSwiney had been arrested six times since his time at Frongoch, and had spent almost two of the four intervening years in jail.

By the time he was sent from the court to jail, MacSwiney was already weak. He vowed to extend his life as long as possible so as to attract the maximum amount of attention, in an attempt to force the authorities to bend. As his health deteriorated, the watching world held its breath, both in horror and in the hope that the authorities would relent. New York dockers threatened strike action, and the Mayor of New York called for MacSwiney's release. In Brazil three hundred thousand Catholics called for the Pope's intervention. In Britain the Labour Party begged the Government to show mercy.

In Jullundur in the Punjab some three hundred and fifty Irish soldiers of the Connaught Rangers laid down their arms on the 25th of June, as a protest against what was happening in Ireland. Of these, sixty-two were court-martialled and sentenced to death, a sentence that was carried out in the case of James Daly. The sentence for the rest was commuted to penal servitude of between two and twenty years.

Worldwide protests continued and, according to official papers released in 2003, King George V himself intervened, only to be told by Lloyd George that releasing MacSwiney could lead to freeing all hunger strikers, whatever their crimes. He said that it would inevitably lead to demolishing law and order and that he could not accept such a responsibility.

The death of Michael Fitzgerald, one of the hunger strikers in Cork Gaol, increased the pressure on the British Goverment. On the seventieth day of his fast, MacSwiney lost consciousness. But even then, such was his determination that he seemed to have conditioned himself to clench his jaws against being forcibly fed. He died at 5.40 a.m. on the 25th of October, the seventy-fourth day of his hunger strike. He was forty years old. Only hours later another Cork Gaol hunger striker died. This was Joseph Murphy. He was just seventeen. On Arthur Griffith's intervention, the remaining hunger strikers then gave up their protest.

The reaction to MacSwiney's death was astounding. Some thirty thousand people paid homage at his coffin as it lay in Southwark Cathedral. Among them was a young British Army officer, Clement Attlee, who would replace Winston Churchill as British Prime Minister within a quarter of a century.

As the Lord Mayor's body was carried through the streets of London on its way to Euston Station for its journey to Holyhead, it was followed by thousands of ordinary citizens, not all of them Irish. Draped over the coffin was the Irish tricolour. In attendance was an escort of Volunteers who openly broke the law by appearing in uniform.

Not all those who wished to pay homage were allowed to do so, however. Micheál Ó Cuill, the man who had walked from Sallins to Dublin to take part in the Rising and who was with MacSwiney in Fron-goch was arrested on the boat on his way over to Holyhead. As the train bearing the Lord Mayor's body passed through Bangor railway station, a number of Welsh students led by Lewis Valentine stood in silent tribute.

It had been planned for MacSwiney's brothers and sisters to meet the train and to transfer their brother's coffin onto a Dublin-bound ferry. There was, however, a last-minute intervention. On the orders of Sir Henry Wilson, the body was not permitted to be taken to Dublin after all. These revised plans had been formulated as the train had approached Crewe. A letter from Sir Hamar Greenwood, the Chief Secretary for Ireland, was handed by a police superintendent to Peter, MacSwiney's brother. The letter informed him that the Government could not allow the body to be taken to Dublin because of the fear of disorder, and that it would be taken directly to Cork City.

At Holyhead the train stopped at the station rather than proceeding to the pier. The passengers were ordered off the train by three hundred policemen who were on board, and by members of the Auxiliaries and the Black and Tans who were on the platform. The travellers were then herded towards a waiting ferry, but some members of the mourning party tried to surround the railway carriage holding the coffin. Despite this protest, the coffin was transferred onto the steamer *Rathmore*. The mourners refused to accompany the coffin on board, and therefore MacSwiney's body left Holyhead Harbour while members of his immediate family prayed at the dockside. An official day of mourning was announced in Cork City and throughout Ireland for the 31st of October, the day of the funeral.

The reaction of the press, both in Britain and elsewhere, was strongly sympathetic. *The Daily Herald* commented: 'The Lord Mayor of Cork is dead. He has his highest reward – the reward of Christ-like service to liberty, the highest of human ideals.' *The Daily Telegraph* remarked: 'The Lord Mayor of Cork condemned himself to death for the sake of a cause in which he passionately believed, and it is impossible for men of decent instincts to think of such an act unmoved.' A French newspaper carried the headline: 'L'Irlande heroique – Bravo Le Lord Mayor de Cork.' The New York Times declared that be it folly or madness, MacSwiney's death was a gesture of deep tragedy acted out on a stage watched by the whole of mankind.

It was the *Daily News*, perhaps, that conveyed the message most succinctly, by stating that 'the Government imprisoned MacSwiney as a criminal and converted him into a martyr and must bear the responsibility for his death'.

Even Asquith, Lloyd George's predecessor, went as far as to say that the decision to allow MacSwiney to die was the biggest political mistake that could have been made. The Lord Mayor's prophecy that his death would be a more effective weapon against the British Empire than his release would ever have been had been realised.

The files relating to MacSwiney's hunger strike have only recently been released. Notes made by Prison Medical Officer W. D. Higson show how much the prisoner suffered even as long as two months before he died. Higson noted how increasingly weak the prisoner was growing. He then noted that MacSwiney had been restless again during the night until 3.00 a.m., and that he had said he felt he was 'drying up'. His heartbeat grew weaker and sometimes missed a beat. Higson recorded that when MacSwiney's physical refusal to take food – meaning his conscious determination not to accept sustenance – had broken down, he, Higson, had insisted in the presence of the priest Father Dominic that every effort should be made to introduce nutritious food into his system so that his life could be prolonged, if not saved.

Taking the path he did, MacSwiney would have been only

too aware of the effect Thomas Ashe's death had had in the eyes of the whole world after his death fast in September 1917. Ashe's action had influenced many others after him. Many ex-Fron-goch internees would again use the hunger strike as a weapon during the War of Independence, including Billy Mullins of the Kerry First Brigade, Tomás Ó Maioileoin, Seán T. O'Kelly and Phil Shanahan.

During the Civil War, ninety-one girls and women undertook a hunger strike in March 1923. During the autumn of 1923, a call was made for three hundred imprisoned Volunteers to begin a hunger strike. Within the first week as many as seven thousand and thirty three had answered the call. On the 28th of October Joseph Whitty of Wexford died in the Curragh. On the 28th of November, Denis Barry of Blackrock in Cork died (in *An Phoblacht*, Wayne Sugg claims that Barry had been at Fron-goch). The Bishop of Cork, Bishop Cohalan, refused to administer the full Christian rites at Barry's funeral. Two days after Barry's death, Andy Sullivan from Mallow died on the fortieth day of his hunger strike at Mountjoy.

The 1930s and 1940s saw similar protests by Republican prisoners. One of the foremost was ex-Fron-goch internee Pat McGrath who was executed in 1940 on de Valera's orders. Earlier the same year, seven IRA prisoners went on hunger strike in protest against the strengthening of the Crime Against the State Act drawn up by Justice Minister Gerry Boland, who was himself an ex-Fron-goch man. Among the seven hunger strikers was Tomás MacCurtain Jr, the son of the former Lord Mayor of Cork. Two of the prisoners, Tony D'Arcy and Seán McNeela both died. MacCurtain Jr had been sentenced to death for shooting a constable but de Valera's Government could not contemplate executing the son of one of the heroes of the Tan War, so his sentence was commuted to that of life imprisonment.

In June 1943, a form of protest that had first been used at

Fron-goch was taken up in Belfast Gaol by twenty-two prisoners who refused to wear prison clothing and went 'on the blanket'. In April 1946 Seán McCaughey died following his hunger strike in Portlaoighise Prison. He refused liquids as well as solids. During the four and a half years he spent in jail, he was forbidden to leave the prison building or even to see the light of day.

In the 1970s the hunger strike became a widespread weapon of protest once more. Among those who made the political headlines were the Price sisters who both spent two hundred and thirteen days on hunger strike and were forcibly fed for a hundred and sixty-six days. They were following the example of members of the 'Cumann na mBan', the women's branch of the IRA, and they included Mary and Annie MacSwiney, Lily Brennan and Nellie Ryan, sister-in-law of Richard Mulcahy, who had been Commander in Chief of the Free State and Defence Minister in February 1923. The strike, which protested against the illegal imprisonment of Republicans, lasted for thirty-four days.

On the 12th of February 1976 Frank Stagg died in Wakefield Gaol following a hunger strike that lasted sixty days – a strike that was a protest for political as opposed to criminal status. In 1980 seven Republican prisoners, three of them women, began a similar protest. Then, between the 5th of May and the 20th of August the following year, these protests reached their climax with no less than ten Republican prisoners dying after fasting for between forty-six and seventy-three days. Three died on the same day. The most prominent among them was Bobby Sands, who died after sixty-six days of refusing food. The others were Francis Hughes (fifty-nine days), Patsy O'Hara (fifty-nine days), Raymond McCreesh (sixty-one days), Joe McDonnell (sixty-one days), Martin Huson (forty-six days), Kevin Lynch (seventy-one days), Kieran Doherty (seventy-three days), Thomas McElwee (sixty-two days) and Michael Devine (sixty days).

The hunger strike continued to be used as a weapon by the Provisional IRA: the Provisional IRA leader Billy McKee led a strike by forty men in Crumlin Road in 1972. IRA Chief of Staff Seán MacStiofáin used the tactic following his arrest in 1973. In 1985 and 1986, and again ten years later, members of INLA (Irish National Liberation Army) adopted similar tactics.

Sean O Mahony stresses that the history of the Irish Republican movement would have been very different without the hunger strike. At Fron-goch there had been many such protests. The highest number to fast all at one time was two hundred. That protest was against conscription, and the camp authorities yielded after only two days.

At Fron-goch Father Stafford, the Camp Chaplain, had tried to persuade the men to forsake such protests on moral and on Catholic religious grounds. This was repeated in 1981 when Cardinal Basil Hume used the same arguments against the H-Block hunger strikers.

The question as to whether the hunger strike is a non-violent means of protesting remains unresolved. In his biography of MacSwiney, Francis J. Costello claims that the Lord Mayor stressed he was dying as a soldier for Ireland:

> When stripped of every last resort, including his freedom, MacSwiney used his body as a weapon against the empire. His hunger strike was an act of protest, but it was not an act of non-violence. By doing violence to himself, MacSwiney sought to do greater harm to Britain.

Costello also emphasises that MacSwiney's fate had been decided from the very first day of his hunger strike. This meant that he had become prisoner of the purity of his own protest:

> By mid-September 1920, realising that the British government would not give in, MacSwiney found himself

hopelessly locked into continuing with his protest. He could not turn back. For a man who had written so much about valour and patriotism, he knew that to do so would be for him a fate worse than death.

MacSwiney's death remains an inspiration to those who fight for justice across the globe. Costello cites the example of Gamsia Kurdia, a member of the Georgian independence movement who was released from prison in Tiblisi in 1990. Kurdia's father had once told Lenin: 'One day, we will have our own MacSwineys and our Casements'. It is said that MacSwiney's sacrifice inspired Mahatma Gandhi in India to revive the custom of 'dbarna', which means 'waiting for death', a Hindu form of the Celtic tradition of fasting, the Troscad.

The irony that is so much a part of Irish history was evident in 1938 when MacSwiney's brother Seán, and MacCurtain's son Tomás MacCurtain Jr were jailed after the passing of yet more stringent legislation against Republican activities by de Valera's government. They appeared in court handcuffed together. The names of MacSwiney and MacCurtain, once linked in life and in death were now linked once more, and both men were still protesting.

10
McKee and Mulcahy

If Michael Collins was destined to become the most notorious of the Fron-goch internees — as well as becoming the most romantic and controversial — he was not by any means the only future leader to emerge from the camp. Collins should be bracketed with two other hugely influential figures who were critical to the future of the Volunteers in the battles that lay ahead: Richard Mulcahy and Dick McKee.

It was Thomas Ashe's death in September 1917 following his hunger strike that led directly to the formation of the General Staff Headquarters of the Volunteers in March 1918. Ashe was one of the heroes of the Easter Rising, second only in importance to de Valera among those who survived. He was sentenced to death but this was commuted and reduced to penal servitude for life. By July 1917, however, he was free and emerged more committed than ever to the cause.

As President of the Irish Republican Brotherhood, he immediately began to reorganise the movement nationally. After an inflammatory speech that he gave in Longford he was arrested under the Defence of the Realm Act for inciting an insurrection, and was sentenced to a year's jail with hard labour. He demanded the right to wear his own clothes and mingle with other prisoners and refused all prison duties. On the 15th of September, as a challenge to the authorities' stubborn refusal to grant him political status, he and six fellow prisoners began their hunger strike. Among them was Tomás Ó Maioleoin, an ex-Fron-goch internee who went under the alias of Seán Forde. He became leader of the West Limerick Brigade and was imprisoned on Beara Island and Spike Island. He managed to escape from Spike with one of Terence

MacSwiney's brothers. During the Civil War he was held at the Curragh and again managed to escape. His brother Séamus was also at Fron-goch.

The reaction of the prison authorities to Ashe's decision to refuse food was to place him in a straitjacket and to force-feed him through a rubber pipe pushed down into his stomach. This clumsy maltreatment led directly to his death after only five days of his hunger strike. The inquest returned a verdict against the prison authorities of acting inhumanely and resorting to dangerous practices.

Ashe's death was manipulated by the leaders of the Volunteers who never failed to take advantage of using publicity as a weapon. The funeral was organised and coordinated by Michael Collins with the assistance of Richard Mulcahy, who had been Ashe's deputy in the Rising. The funeral procession included eighteen thousand trade unionists and nine thousand Volunteers.

Mulcahy had distinguished himself in the Rising. On the Sunday evening he was sent by James Connolly to Howth to cut the telephone wires between Dublin and London. Finding it impossible to return to the city, he went to Ashbourne to the north of Dublin to join up with Ashe who was preparing an attack on the police barracks. The barracks were successfully taken, but sixty police reserves arrived and Ashe and his men were outnumbered. Nevertheless, Mulcahy used a clever ruse to fool the police into thinking that the Volunteers were numerous, when in fact there were only seven of them. This small crew rushed at the police and scattered them.

Mulcahy's next task was to travel to Kilmainham Gaol where he sought confirmation of the general surrender. He received the message of surrender directly from Pearse himself. On the 17th of June Mulcahy was sent from Knutsford to Fron-goch, where he was put in charge of Company D and appointed Officer in Charge of Dormitory 3. He was also appointed Lieutenant. Following the general release he was appointed Commandant of the Dublin Second Battalion and then Commandant of the Dublin Brigade. He subsequently became Director of Training of the Volunteers. Because of his part in the Rising, he lost his job with the Post Office, and turned to studying medicine at University College Dublin. Throughout the Tan War he was Chief of Staff of the National Executive although Cathal Brugha was regarded by many as holding that position until March 1919.

In 1918 Mulcahy was elected TD for Clontarf and he went on to become Dáil Éirann's first Defence Minister. It was Mulcahy, aided by Brugha, who managed to persuade the Volunteers to act under Dáil orders. After the Civil War he was appointed Defence Minister in Government and Army Chief of Staff. Some of his officials were responsible for executing many ex-comrades both during and after the Civil War. Later in his career he was appointed Minister for Education and Public Health, and he became Leader of Fine Gael.

Mulcahy married Josephine Ryan, whose brother Dr James Ryan was interned with him at Fron-goch. Ryan had treated the injured James Connolly, and at Fron-goch he shared a hut with Collins. After his release he won a seat for Sinn Féin in South Wexford in 1918. He was interned on Spike Island and at Hare Internment Camp.

The Ryan family fiercely opposed the Treaty. Ryan was appointed Minister for Finance in de Valera's Fianna Fáil government. Phyllis, another of Ryan's sisters, married Seán T. O'Kelly, who was also in Fron-goch. Yet another, Nellie, was one of twenty-three members of Cumann na mBan who went on hunger strike in 1923.

Like Mulcahy, Dick McKee played a prominent role in the 1916 Rebellion. He is perhaps the least appreciated of the military leaders created by the Rising, but he should be regarded as possibly the greatest among those who reorganised the Volunteers, turning them from the beaten rabble of Easter 1916 into a well-drilled and disciplined army.

Born in Phibsborough Road in Dublin and raised in Finglas Bridge, he was a printer by trade with Gill and Sons. He fought under MacDonagh during Easter Week and, as a young man of twenty-three, he proved his worth when he faced an angry mob outside Jacob's. He confronted the infuriated Dublin citizens on his own, and through reasoned argument managed to earn their respect. He and his men at Jacob's were among the last to surrender. Such was the impression made by McKee and his men that they were given a rousing reception as they were marched away by the British military. On the 3rd of May, he was sent to Knutsford and then on to Fron-goch.

McKee was released in August 1916 and when members of the General Staff Headquarters were elected in March 1918 Richard Mulcahy was chosen ahead of Collins as Chief of Staff. McKee was honest enough to tell Collins himself that he had too impetuous a nature for such a post. Collins was chosen as Deputy Director of Organisation and Adjutant-General because, as McKee had suggested, many believed he should be groomed under the wing of someone of a steadier nature. Mulcahy fitted the bill. This meant that Collins was able to turn his attention to other important activities.

McKee was elected Director of Training. Another ex-Fron-goch internee, Seán McMahon, was elected Quartermaster General. Rory O'Connor as Director of Engineering was the fifth of the five principal officers. Four of the five officers immediately in charge of directing military activities were ex-Fron-goch internees. Tragically and ironically, the Fron-goch connection would play a part in the death of the odd man out, Rory O'Connor. He was executed in December 1922 with three other Republicans on the orders of Mulcahy, for his part in shooting dead Seán Hales, who had also been in Fron-goch.

Collins, Mulcahy and McKee will always be bracketed

together, not only because of their feats, but also because of their physical presence. Ulick O'Connor notes that poet and surgeon Oliver St John Gogarty had described Collins as being

…Napoleonic. But a bigger and more manly specimen of manhood than Napoleon…. His skin was like undiscoloured ivory. You could see it in the unlined face and beautiful womanly hands.

Mulcahy, with his small, lithe frame, his thoughtful look and suggestion of powerful inner energy, bore a marked resemblance to T. E. Lawrence, the leader of the Arab revolt.

McKee was the tallest of the three. He was over six feet tall, broad shouldered, and had the easy carriage of an athlete. O'Connor claims that

… the distinctive qualities which were to make the alliance between the three so successful were their gifts of organisation. Nothing could send Collins into a fury more than the easy-going approach of some of his comrades. One of his sayings was, 'We must stick to the facts if we are to achieve anything in life', while a maxim of McKee's was, 'Efficiency eliminates chance'. Mulcahy was so devoted to the work ethic that he could make himself unwell if even a minor hitch occurred in an enterprise he was involved with, such as a slip in a time schedule or someone failing to turn up.

According to O'Connor, the three of them formed the perfect team:

The partnership of the three would prove dynamic. Later, Collins, as Director of Intelligence, was to create a unique network which would provide a model for guerrilla groups throughout the rest of this century. McKee, as the general in the field, acted on information supplied through the secret army which he trained with the same fierce efficiency as his colleagues demonstrated in their own areas of operations. Mulcahy quietly created the conditions through which the combination of the three could best work. From now on the IRB was basically on a war footing – waiting for the chance they knew must come, when they would unleash the Volunteers against the forces that would oppose them.

During this period of reconstruction, McKee was the key figure. According to O'Connor, it was McKee who was the architect of the method of fighting that was described by the British as ditch-murder. Later on, Mao Tse Tung in China, Tito in Yugoslavia, General Giap in Vietnam, Che Guevara in Central America and Nelson Mandela in South Africa would adopt exactly the same tactics. O'Connor could also have added the name of George Grivas, the leader of EOKA, the guerrilla army that fought for independence for Cyprus in the mid-1950s, as well as the names of Menachem Begin and Yitzak Shamir, two of the Irgun underground movement in British Mandate Palestine during the 1940s. Both would go on to become Prime Ministers of Israel. Indeed, Tim Pat Coogan claims that while fighting in the Israeli underground army, Shamir adopted the alias 'Micail' as a tribute to Collins. Begin likewise was a great admirer, as he revealed in his autobiography *The Revolt*.

The success of the Flying Columns of the Volunteers, particularly Tom Barry's massacre of the Auxiliaries at Kilmichael on the 28th of November 1920, would echo round the world. It became required reading at military academies such as Sandhurst and West Point. It is said that the German army studied Barry's tactics during the Second World War, and in *The IRA and its Enemies* Peter Hart cites an unsubstantiated story that the Japanese army marched into Singapore singing 'The Boys of Kilmichael'. Ironically, the man who had ignominiously surrendered Singapore to the Japanese was

Major Percival, who had been in command of the Essex Regiment based in West Cork during the Tan War. He was described by Tom Barry as 'easily the most viciously anti-Irish of all serving British officers. He was tireless in his attempts to destroy the spirit of the people and the organisation of the IRA'. It is not difficult to imagine the chagrin he would have felt if he had witnessed the enemy's marching song: it would have reminded him of his previous failure in Ireland.

The IRA's tactics are still standard learning for guerrillas world-wide. Indeed, as recently as January 2004, a leading press defence correspondent traced the terrorist tactics used against police recruits in Iraq all the way back to those devised and used by the IRA in Ireland between 1916 and 1921:

> The IRA sought to make Ireland ungovernable and chose the Royal Irish Constabulary as the primary target. Initially this attracted much opposition from the Irish themselves as officers of the RIC were almost all Catholic.

The correspondent observes that enlisting was a common means of escape for younger sons of Catholic farmers, young men who became a burden on the income of small farms, and he points out that the IRA began by attacking solitary country police posts where the constables and their families lived, which forced them into the towns.

Almost ninety years after the Rising this newspaper correspondent traces the guerrilla tactics used in Iraq directly back to Collins, Mulcahy and McKee and, although the writer does not realise it, all the way back to Fron-goch. Between 1919 and 1922, a total of six hundred and eighteen policemen were killed in Ireland, which is almost ten times the number of British soldiers killed during the same period.

McKee, in particular, became a thorn in the side of the British authorities. He was responsible for an unsuccessful attempt on the life of Lord French, British Governor in Ireland. He had a direct link to the Big Four, Seán Treacy, Dan Breen, Seán Hogan and Séamus Robinson, and had a narrow escape when Treacy was shot dead in Talbot Street in 1920. When Breen was severely wounded and was apparently on his deathbed, it was McKee who led the crew who managed to snatch him, transfer him to the Mater Hospital, and guard him there while British troops were searching for him.

Collins had organised a propaganda department to work hand in hand with his intelligence organisation, and it was led by Desmond Fitzgerald and the journalist Piaras Béaslaí. When Béaslaí, Rory O'Connor and J. J. Walsh were arrested, McKee was responsible for rescuing them from Mountjoy Prison. Although he was deeply involved in the action, he still found time to print the Republican newspaper *An-tÓglach* from a secret base in Aungier Street.

McKee was eventually captured during his planning of the infamous Bloody Sunday attack. On the 20th of November 1920 he met with Collins, Mulcahy and Pedar Clancy in Phil Shanahan's bar in the Gloucester Diamond. Shanahan, a Tipperary man, was a Fron-goch graduate who had organised a gang of newspaper delivery boys to work as spies for Collins. He had been a prominent hunger striker and would go on to be an anti-Treaty TD.

Present that night in Shanahan's Bar was a British spy. He followed McKee and Clancy to a safe house, which was the home of Seán Fitzpatrick in Gloucester Street, and passed the information on to the British authorities in Dublin Castle. McKee was carrying incriminating documents that named the secret agents who were targeted to be shot the following morning. He managed to burn the evidence just before he was arrested. He and Clancy were taken to Dublin Castle and were thrown in a cell that was already occupied by a young man, Conor Clune, who had no connection whatsoever with the

Volunteers. He was an Irish-language enthusiast who was up in Dublin for the football match that was to be played at Croke Park on that Sunday afternoon.

The prisoners were interrogated by Captains Hardy and King, both of whom were well known for their cruel methods of extracting information. All three prisoners were stabbed with bayonets, but McKee and Clancy would not reveal anything. Poor Clune could not have revealed anything even if he had wished to, as he knew absolutely nothing about the impending action. After more stabbings and after having had their fingernails torn out, all three were shot dead. According to the authorities they were shot while trying to escape, but this hardly tallies with the fact that Clune had been shot thirteen times. The whole shameful episode is recorded in Sean O Mahony's pamphlet *Three Murders in Dublin Castle*.

When Collins heard about the deaths he was overcome with rage. McKee in particular had been very close to him. As the bodies lay in the Pro Cathedral he demonstrated his legendary recklessness by pushing his way past the watching soldiers and dressing McKee and Clancy in their military uniforms. During the memorial service, under the very noses of the enemy, he stepped forward and left a note on the coffins that stated: 'In memory of two good friends – Dick and Peadar – and two of Ireland's best soldiers. Miceal O'Coilleain, 25/11/1920.' He helped carry the coffins to the hearse on their way to Glasnevin Cemetery. At McKee's side throughout that last journey was another old comrade from Fron-goch, Batt O'Connor.

If historians seem to have been averse to paying McKee his due for the part he played in Irish history, Collins nevertheless recognised his importance. After the funeral he poured out his heart to Batt O'Connor who quotes him as saying:

It will be almost impossible to find a man to fill his place.

There was no one like him for the thoroughness with which he made all the arrangements for carrying out a difficult or dangerous undertaking. He never overlooked the smallest detail. And you know, Batt, in our fight, to fail to foresee everything, and arrange for everything, means disaster. I always consulted him on my own plans before I put them into execution. He was my right-hand man in arranging all the details for the escape of our men from the prisons. I would first submit to him all my arrangements for any action I proposed to take, then and then only would I go on with our work. Such was the great soldier you have laid to rest today, and who had so small a funeral.

McKee was succeeded as Chief Officer of the Dublin Brigade by Oscar Traynor, who was another Fron-goch graduate. He was responsible for leading the attack on the Customs House on the 25th of May 1921. A member of Fianna Fáil, he served later as Defence Minister.

The story of McKee and Clancy's betrayal does not end with their funeral, however. Phil Shanahan managed to track down the man who had betrayed them that night in the bar. Bill Stapleton was summoned, and the traitor was taken in Haynes' tavern in Gloucester Place and shot. His body was left at The Five Lamps nearby. In a conversation with Ulick O'Connor, Stapleton recalled: 'He was a strong man and tried to deny his part.'

The traitor was an ex-military policeman, James Ryan. Ryan was the son (or, according to Dan Breen, the brother) of Becky Cooper, who kept one of Dublin's most infamous brothels and who was immortalised in Dominic Behan's song 'Dicey Riley'. The novelist Liam O'Flaherty was a frequenter of Dicey Riley's place and it was on this episode of retribution that he based his famous novel *The Informer*, which was later adapted as a film.

Mulcahy's importance has been more generally

acknowledged than that of McKee. During his internment at Fron-goch he had already shown that he had the pedigree that fitted him to be a future leader. Séamas Ó Maoileoin recalled one particular incident in the camp involving an argument as to what should happen after the prisoners' release. Mulcahy's answer was unambiguous:

> Freedom will never come without a revolution, but I fear Irish people are too soft for that. To have a real revolution, you must have bloody fierce-minded men who do not care a scrap for death or bloodshed. A real revolution is not a job for children, or for saints or scholars. In the course of revolution, any man, woman or child who is not with you is against you. Shoot them and be damned to them.

He was to remain true to those sentiments both in his fight against the British and against his former comrades during the Civil War.

Despite his adherence to the cause, Mulcahy was not a member of the Irish Republican Brotherhood and, according to Maryann Gialanella Valiulis, his relationship with Collins at Fron-goch was never a close one. In her biography of Mulcahy, Valiulis claims that he tended to consider himself an outsider and he was never invited to the IRB meetings. But in a debate on the Constitution in the Dáil on the 16th of October 1931 Gerry Boland offered a different story. He accused Mulcahy, together with Gearóid O'Sullivan and Collins of stealthily bringing the IRB into the Irish army stating:

> I sat with you at the same meeting in Frongoch when you reorganised it and I was invited by you and by Mick Collins and I would not go. I know you are one of the people who started the whole damn thing in Frongoch, you and the bunch around you. You started the false propaganda in the place. I organised a group of truthful men who would not

sign a lying statement. You and a few others organised this thing and passed this cursed Treaty.

He went on to accuse Mulcahy of suggesting that British troops should be poisoned, and described him as the reincarnation of Cromwell.

At the time, Mulcahy was Minister for Local Government and Public Health, while Boland was TD for Fianna Fáil. Before very long, Boland would be Justice Minister responsible for signing the death warrants of Republicans, at least one of whom had been with him in Fron-goch.

Valiulis asserts that it was in Fron-goch that Mulcahy 'experienced the type of organisation and solidarity which made prison such an important and radicalizing experience for so many of the prisoners'. Beside his military successes, and the ignominy of his having treated Republicans during the Civil War with the same mercilessness as the British Government had used, Mulcahy will also be remembered for the eulogy he gave at the graveside of his old comrade, Michael Collins:

> We bend over the grave of a man not more than thirty years of age, who took to himself the gospel of toil for Ireland, the gospel of working for the people of Ireland, and of sacrifice for their good.... Unless the grain of corn that falls into the ground died, there is nothing but itself in it, but if it dies, it gives forth great truth.... 'Prophecy', said Peter, who was the great rock, 'is a light shining in the darkness till the day dawns' ... and surely, our great rock was our prophet and our prophecy, a light held aloft along the road of danger or hardship or bitter toil. And if our light is gone out it is only as the paling of a candle in the dawn of its own prophecy.... Men and women of Ireland, we are all mariners on the deep, bound for a port still seen only through storm and spray, sailing on a sea full of dangers

and hardships and bitter toil. But the Great Sleeper lies smiling in the stern of the boat, and we shall be filled with that spirit which will walk bravely upon the waters.

As far as Mulcahy was concerned, Collins could do no wrong. James Ryan, Mulcahy's brother-in-law, is quoted in the Ernie O'Malley Papers as having said that 'no matter what Mick Collins said, Dick Mulcahy thought he was right. Mulcahy took no credit for anything. Always Mick was the big man with him'.

It was appropriate, therefore, that Mulcahy should step into the breach left by Collins. He would be the only member of the original General Staff Headquarters to die of natural causes. Valiulis quotes John A. Costello who described him as a man who had served his country well without being fully appreciated. 'I personally have never come across any man who was so selfless in public or national affairs,' he added.

In 1971 I contacted Mulcahy to enquire about his recollections of his time at Fron-goch. He was then eighty-five years old. Knowing he was not well, I was surprised to receive a reply. He did not wish to elaborate on his time in Fron-goch, but he did pass on some important research sources. He died in December that year.

11
Legacy

What happened at Fron-goch has left its mark on countless individuals and on world history. Colonel Frederick Arthur Heygate-Lambert, the Camp Commandant, was made redundant on the 8th of January 1917 after the release of the men. He remained in the area, residing at Bod-eryl, Dolgellau. He was later involved in a dispute as to which rank he could claim at the end of the war, and spent the rest of his army days as a temporary major in the Labour Corps, and on the general list as Major, but graded as Staff Lieutenant Second Class. He died in April 1919.

No less than thirty Fron-goch men were TDs, or Members of the Irish Parliament, at the time of the Treaty in December 1921, and in terms of their allegiance they were split down the middle. On the Free State side these included Michael Collins, Richard Mulcahy, Michael Staines, Seán Hales and Joe Sweeney. Among the Republican TDs were Brian O'Higgins, Dr James Ryan, Phil Shanahan, Séamus Robinson and Seán T. O'Kelly.

Joe Connolly, Seán Gibbons, Séamus Fitzgerald and Séamus Robinson were among those who became Senators, members of the Upper House. Others who made their mark included Cathal O'Shannon, who became Vice-President of the Irish Labour Party; Michael Lynch, who became chief of the Translation Staff of the Oireachtas (both Houses of Parliament); Pádraig Ó Caoimh, who became Acting Governor of Mountjoy Prison, when four prisoners under his charge were executed without trial; Seán Nunan, Irish Minister to the US and later Secretary of the Department of External Affairs (Foreign); his brother Ernest, who was one of four clerks in the First Dáil; Joseph Lawless, Director of Cavalry in the Free State Army; Eamonn Bulfin, Irish Consul to Argentina; Thomas Derrig, Minister of Education; Thomas Harris, Chairman of Kildare County Council; Séamus Murphy, Dublin City Commissioner, and Oscar Traynor, Minister for Defence.

Michael Brennan of County Clare was the first of the Fron-goch internees to adopt the tactic of not acknowledging the legitimacy of the court before which he stood. He became Chief of Staff of the National Army. Seán T. O'Kelly became TD for Mid-Dublin in 1918, and was in charge of the Irish Office in Paris. He was opposed to the Treaty and joined de Valera in Fianna Fáil, becoming Minister for Local Government and Finance and later President of Ireland.

In 1920 eight Fron-goch graduates were among the thirteen officers who made up the IRA General Headquarters Staff. As well as Richard Mulcahy (Chief of Staff), J. J. O'Connell (Assistant Chief of Staff), Dick McKee (Officer Commanding, Dublin Brigade), and Michael Collins (Director of Intelligence), there were Gearóid O'Sullivan (Adjutant General); Eamon Price (Director of Organisation); Seán Russell (Director of Munitions), and Sean MacMahon (Quartermaster General).

During the Civil War, almost twenty ex-Fron-goch internees achieved senior rank in the Free State Army. They were Michael Collins (Commander in Chief); Richard Mulcahy (Chief of Staff and later Commander in Chief); Sean MacMahon (Chief of the General Staff); Gearóid O'Sullivan (Adjutant General); J. J. O'Connell (Lieutenant General); Michael Brennan (General Officer Commanding Limerick); Peadar MacMahon (General Officer Commanding Curragh); Paddy Daly (General Officer Commanding Kerry); Joe Sweeney (General Officer Commanding Donegal); Tom Ennis (Major General Officer Commanding 2nd Eastern Division); Seán Guilfoyle (Major General I/C Staff Duties), as well as

Seán Boylan, Fred Henry, Eamon Morkan, Joe O'Reilly, James Shiels, Joseph Lawless and James Slattery (Colonels and Senior Officers). To these could be added Michael Staines and Paddy Brennan, Commissioner and Assistant Commissioner respectively of the Gárda Síochána, the Irish Police Force.

Among Fron-goch ex-internees to be killed during the Civil War were M. J. Ring and Hugh Thornton and another was Paddy O'Brien, a Republican. In 1924 O'Brien's brother, Denis, who was also at Fron-goch, was shot dead outside his own home by Republicans.

J. J. O'Connell, the first Officer in Command to be held at Fron-goch, became Assistant Director of Training in 1920, before he succeeded Dick McKee as Director. During the Truce between the end of the War of Independence and the signing of the Treaty, he was Chief of Staff of the IRA, and was later appointed to a similar rank in the Free State Army.

One lasting legacy of Fron-goch is the New Ireland Assurance company. The idea for such an organisation was mooted at Fron-goch and the first meeting of what was initially called the New Ireland Assurance Collecting Society was held at the home of ex-internee Tom Sinnott, before the company was founded in 1918. During the War of Independence its offices were used as Sinn Féin headquarters, and every member of staff was an IRA officer. The company, which is now allied to the Bank of Ireland and has its headquarters in Dawson Street in Dublin, has nineteen branches nationwide. Five of its founders were at Fron-goch: M. W. O'Reilly, Denis McCullough (Mac Con Uladh), James Ryan, Tomás Ó Nualláin and Michael Staines. Other Fron-goch men involved were F. X. Coughlan, Michael Lynch, Joe Doherty and Hugh Thornton.

A much less admirable Fron-goch legacy that remains is the practice of internment. It was Brian O'Higgins who, looking back at his own incarceration, described internment as 'the most terrible of all "humane" punishment'. Internment, which began some fifteen years before the Irish arrived at Fron-goch Camp still continues long after it. In the Foreword to his book *Frongoch: University of Revolution* Sean O Mahony observes that it was Lord Kitchener, an Irishman from County Kerry, who was the founder of the first ever internment camp. During the Boer War he was responsible for the rounding up of 'hostile natives' in South Africa and holding them in stockades. O Mahony remarks:

> Conditions in these camps were appalling and the internees died in large numbers. However the system has been refined somewhat and has been used extensively in this century by the British, Six-County and 26 County administrations both in the UK and in Ireland.

As a result of internment, almost twenty-eight thousand Boer civilians, most of them women and children, died from measles and typhus epidemics that ran unchecked through the camps in 1901. This was more than the total number of combatants killed on both sides of the war. Three-quarters of those who died were children under the age of sixteen. The total number of civilians who died in separate black camps was some twenty thousand. O Mahony observes:

> The name of Long Kesh has now entered the nomenclature of dreadful places from the present generation and it is very much alive in the minds of politicised people. Long Kesh was the last place where Irish internees were held on this island in 1974. However, the first use of a concentration camp by the British for Irish political prisoners was at Frongoch, a small valley in North Wales, in the period after the Rebellion in 1916. During a recent visit to Frongoch a Welsh lady said to me: 'and imagine, I thought only the

Germans had concentration camps'.

O Mahony's book was published in 1987, and it was in part the apathy of the Irish Government during the seventieth anniversary of the Rising in 1986 that motivated him to write it. The book followed an essay that he had previously written on Fron-goch, with which he meant to show how this internment camp in Wales had had a major impact on Irish history. O Mahony regards that impact as being threefold. Firstly, it was the first All Ireland Republican convention:

> Volunteers virtually from all parts of Ireland were brought together and from this melting pot emerged the revitalised Irish Republican Army. They proceeded to engage the British Government with its vast resources, human, industrial and military in a war of liberation. This led at its conclusion to the withdrawal of the British from 26 counties of Ireland and this defection was clearly the first major crack in the Empire.

Secondly, he states that the Irish Republican Brotherhood was successfully reorganised in Fron-goch, and that 'Many of those destined to play a major role in the events leading to the foundation of the Free State were recruited in the camp to this secret revolutionary body.' Thirdly, he states that the policy of Irish prisoners of war towards their captors was first formulated in Fron-goch, when the issue of political status was contested vigorously:

> The British resolved the issue by giving a de facto political status just as William Whitelaw did in 1972 in the Six Counties when he granted 'Special Category' status to the IRA prisoners.

Like O Mahony, John McGuffin emphasises in *Internment*

that it was the Boer War that gave the world the name 'concentration camp', bringing shame and ignominy to Britain, 'which was accustomed for so long to have her imperialist way without question'. He observes that during the nineteenth century alone as many as a hundred and five Coercion Bills were passed, Bills that meant, to all intent and purposes, the imprisonment of Irish people. He notes that between 1881 and 1882 over one thousand Irish people were imprisoned without warrant, accusation or a court hearing. They were merely under suspicion. The right to Habeas Corpus was suspended and these conditions led to the formation of the Land League.

The internment camps, however, were something entirely new. He believes that Fron-goch, where the men in both of the camps elected their own leaders and established a chain of command, set a precedent. He lists the many mistakes made by the British, including the execution of the leaders and the attempt to conscript the 'refugees', but claims that the worst mistake was to use internment in the first place, as the camps became 'hotbeds of sedition, political education centres and training grounds for resistance fighters'. McGuffin also maintains that it was a mistake to end internment at Fron-goch so soon: 'First, martyrs had been made, then the survivors were turned loose to an admiring audience.'

According to McGuffin, by the Truce of 1921 there were seven thousand Irish political prisoners in the jails of England and Ireland (including, presumably, Wales and Scotland), many of whom were held on ridiculous charges, such as whistling derisively or carrying a hurley. The Defence of the Realm Act was used extensively, and special Irish Clauses were periodically added. On the 24th of April 1918, for example, DORA was quietly altered to allow the authorities to take Irish prisoners to be interned in England. Even after the Treaty, over a hundred Irish men and women were interned in Ireland. Most of these were members of the Self-Determination League who were later released because they had been unlawfully interned.

McGuffin gives an account of the various internment camps established by Britain in Aden, Cyprus, Malaya, and especially in Kenya. In Kenya, eleven members of the Mau Mau were beaten to death at Hola Camp on the 24th of February 1959, and over eighty thousand were interned without charge, while some seven hundred were kept captive for over seven years.

Before the Second World War, Britain once more introduced internment, and again the internees were Irish, although German and Italian citizens, many of them refugees in Britain, were also interned in 'enemy alien' camps during the war. McGuffin points out that the internment of Irish people followed the ill-conceived IRA bombing campaign in England led by Sean Russell, another ex-Fron-goch man, who died on board a German submarine off the Galway coast in 1940. He was in the company of Frank Ryan, a left-wing Republican who had led a contingent of Irishmen against Franco's forces during the Spanish Civil War. Russell was a staff officer and was elected Director of Munitions on Staff Headquarters in 1921. He was responsible for organising the quarry raid that precipitated the War of Independence, and he became Chief of Staff of the IRA in 1938. His bombing campaign led to the execution of two Volunteers, Barnes and McCormack, and over a hundred Irish people were jailed.

Among the many government leaders who condemned internment at first, only to embrace it later, McGuffin lists Makarios, Banda, Nehru, Gandhi and de Valera. He observes that what made this hypocrisy worse was the fact that these leaders had themselves suffered from the effects of internment. All of them went on to become respectable politicians.

For the Irish, internment returned in 1971. The *Insight* team of journalists who worked for the *Sunday Times* in 1972 came to the conclusion that politicians had been well aware that adopting an internment policy in the Six Counties would be a mistake, as such a move would merely promote more violence and would further alienate Catholics. The journalists produced statistics to prove their point: during the four months prior to the adoption of internment, four soldiers had been killed. During the four months after internment was introduced, between August and November 1971, thirty soldiers, eleven police officers and seventy-three ordinary citizens were killed. By mid-December that year, more than fifteen hundred had been arrested under the Special Powers Act, almost all of whom were Catholics. *Insight's* contention was that rather than easing the situation, internment had served only to drive Catholics who had until then been neutral into the arms of the IRA.

The lessons of Fron-goch, it seems, had either been forgotten or never learned in the first place by the British, but the lessons taught to the men of Fron-goch by their own leaders would be learned and remembered by many other countries, nations and factions. The hit-and-run tactics used during the Tan War became the gospel of revolutionaries worldwide. In *The Black and Tans* Richard Bennett points out that in the first year of its war against England, the IRA had killed at most twenty-six people, eighteen of them policemen, and had fired shots on not much more than a hundred occasions. He maintains that no government would capitulate to such a threat.

However, in *The War of the Flea: A Study of Guerrilla Warfare*, Robert Taber corrects what he considers to be a misconception on the part of Bennett and states: 'The fact is that England *did* capitulate, if not to the threat *per se*, then to the intolerable political and economic situation that it was to produce, given another year.' Taber's most interesting assertion is that the IRA was not fighting a military war but, rather, a political war, and that the true effects of the terror were psychological and political. Much of the IRA's action, he maintains, was only nuisance value:

> Newspaper ink flowed more freely than blood. IRA gunmen missed more often than hit their targets. The barracks that burned were often empty and their destruction only symbolic; often, too, the raiders were repulsed, having expended more ammunition than they had hoped to capture, and the victims of the gunmen were more frequently Irish than English – suspected informers, collaborators and the like.

Taber maintains that the IRA never gained sufficient strength to defeat the British military forces in any engagement of any size:

> Although the British Viceroy, Lord French, estimated it as some 100,000 strong and the British Secretary for Ireland doubled the estimate, reporting an army of 200,000, 'ready to murder by day and night', its peak strength, on paper, was never more than 15,000 men, and Michael Collins later put the effective fighting strength of the IRA at 3,000.

It was Collins himself who said: 'All I want to lead is sixty determined trustworthy men, and I'll beat the British.' What helped turn the tide was propaganda. Taber regards the arrival of the Black and Tans as a godsend to the IRA:

> For every incident the latter produced, the former produced another, and where the actions of the IRA could be admired abroad, as part of a courageous struggle for liberty, the reprisals of the Tans could only draw blame – and further unite the Irish in opposition to the Crown.

What Taber does not acknowledge is that it was at Frongoch that the twin forces of Irish revolution were created and theorised before they were put into practice during the Tan War. It was at Fron-goch that the blueprint for small, mobile, hard-hitting and quick-retreating armed groups, coupled with clever propaganda and intelligence, was formed.

In this respect, internment is not the only link between the Boers and Fron-goch, because it was the Boers who had pioneered the methods that were so efficiently streamlined by the Irish internees at Fron-goch. When the British took control of several Boer towns at the end of 1900, some Boer commando units refused to lay down their arms. They escaped into the bush and waged a guerrilla war against the British using ambush methods. They lived off the land and kept to terrain they knew, using hit-and-run tactics and capturing British weapons. Returning Irish soldiers such as Seán McBride or Jack White who trained the Irish Citizen Army had fought with the Boers and brought back with them the rudiments of what would be perfected at Fron-goch.

In his essay 'The Black Hand' Jon Parry observes of the Fron-goch internees:

Their brief sojourn in rural Wales nurtured the seeds of modern Ireland. The name Frongoch has resonated through the decades as one of the symbols of the revolutionary period in Ireland. It was one of the few Welsh names with which Irish people were familiar, even if they found it unpronounceable. Similarly ... to some Welsh men and women it became a symbol of national struggle ...

Parry, however, asserts that Fron-goch has been given a significance that it does not merit. Many Irish historians, from Tim Pat Coogan to Peter Hart, would disagree.

Fron-goch remains a link in a chain that stretches from South Africa in 1899 through Long Kesh, Magilligan and Maghaberry Prison in the 1970s, to Belmarsh and Guantanamo Bay at the beginning of the twenty-first century.

Indeed, in the autumn of 2005 some two hundred internees at Guantanamo Bay began a hunger strike that echoes some of the events at Fron-goch.

While it was his conviction that the camp had played an important role in Irish history that motivated Sean O Mahony to write *Frongoch: University of Revolution*, he could well have claimed that the camp had played an important role in world history. Fron-goch was a geographical accident: had the Irish not been detained there, they would have been detained somewhere else, but it was Fron-goch that was chosen. Had it not been for Fron-goch, would Collins have become such an important figure? Would Richard Mulcahy, Dick McKee, Tomás MacCurtain and Terence MacSwiney have played such prominent roles? Had it not been for Collins, Mulcahy, McKee, MacCurtain and MacSwiney, would the world have heard so much about Mao Tse Tung, Tito, General Giap, Che Guevara, Nelson Mandela and Menachem Begin?

It is not mere conjecture to link Fron-goch to such important figures in world history. In *The IRA at War 1916-1923* Peter Hart observes:

> Irish republicans invented revolutionary warfare, with its mass parties, popular fronts, guerrilla warfare, underground governments, and continuous propaganda campaigns. What Michael Collins and company did in post-Great War Ireland, Mao, Tito and Ho Chi Minh would do during and after the next world war. Irish rebels did not know they were doing this, however, so no patent was claimed. The formula for success had to be reinvented and would be exported by more pragmatic strategists. Thus, comparative students of revolution have passed Ireland by as well. It has not found its place alongside France, Russia, China, Cuba, and Iran in the analytical pantheon.

As far as Fron-goch is concerned, it is difficult to avoid Joe

Good's conclusion as he looked back on Christmas 1916. He believed that the British had little or no choice but to release the remaining internees. Britain announced that the men were being released as a gesture of conciliation, but Good claims that the men themselves knew the real reason:

> We knew we had bit the hand that fed us so badly it was glad to release us. The men all believed, and they were proven right in this, that they had irrevocably intimidated Whitehall and Downing Street.

The internees had been sent to an internment camp rather than to various British jails because, as Jon Parry notes in 'The Black Hand', they had not been deemed important enough to be sent to jails such as Hereford, Portland, Knutsford and Dartmoor. It was during their stay at Fron-goch that they became important:

> Frongoch would now enter Irish mythology and the men who had languished here became a part of a hierarchy of the revolutionary tradition .... For a few short months in 1916 the greatest concentration of Irish revolutionaries in modern times were incarcerated in north Wales. It was in Meirioneth that a brief period of internment laid the ground for the War of Independence, the Civil War, the creation of the Free State.... British exigency had resulted in a bleak and desolate Welsh upland becoming a focal point for revolutionary ardour, national symbolism, youthful energy and cultural commitment. The heroic march of modern Irish history ended with the assassination of Collins in the lovely valley of Béal nBleath in West Cork; it may have begun on the dreary slopes near Bala in north Wales.

12

Epilogue

In 1955, Liverpool Corporation announced its plans to present a Private Bill to Parliament requesting the right to build a dam across the Tryweryn river at Capel Celyn. By 1960 the Irish had returned to Fron-goch. This time they were there voluntarily to build the dam that would supply Liverpool with Welsh water. With jobs scarce in Ireland, there was work to be done and money to be earned in the very place where almost half a century earlier their fathers, uncles and grandfathers had dreamed of freedom.

There was much opposition to the scheme. On the 24th of September 1956 the campaigners received a letter of support:

When against terrific odds a small nation is seeking to preserve its personality and culture the destruction of any area where the language and national characteristics have been traditionally preserved would be a misfortune which every effort should be made to avoid.

Material economic advantages are far too dearly bought when secured at the loss of an inspiring spiritual inheritance and some modern efficiency enthusiasts need to have this fact forcibly impressed upon them.

When alternatives which do not involve such a loss are available, all who believe that man has needs other than those of the body will sympathise with the people of the Welsh nation in their efforts to see the alternatives to the Tryweryn scheme be found and adopted. I wish you every success.

The letter was signed Eamon de Valera, Dáil Éireann, Dublin.

At the Bill's second reading not one Welsh Member of Parliament voted for the scheme. Some, however, for various reasons decided to abstain or withhold their vote. One of these was Megan Lloyd George, whose father had supported the visit to Blaenau Ffestiniog of Michael Davitt from the Land League in 1885, who had freed the last of the Fron-goch internees in 1916, and who had been instrumental in dividing Ireland in 1921. Eirene White was another Welsh MP who supported Liverpool Corporation's call for drowning Tryweryn. Her father, Thomas Jones, had been Personal Secretary to Lloyd George. A small group of other Welsh MPs expressed a range of opinions from open support for Liverpool to downright indifference. Among the latter was that great champion of the oppressed, Aneurin Bevan.

These were exceptions, however, for the great majority of opinion was overwhelmingly against the drowning of Capel Celyn. The Welsh David turned out to be no match for the bullying Goliath of Liverpool, however, backed as it was by a large number of English MPs. The local Bala Town Council twisted the knife by giving its blessing to the scheme.

Frustration led some young Welshmen to take the law into their own hands. On the 22nd of September 1962 two Monmouthshire men, David Pritchard and David Walters, sabotaged an electric transformer on the site by draining it of oil. They were arrested, but sympathetic magistrates merely fined them £50 each.

On Sunday the 10th of February 1963 a far more serious incident occurred, when a mains transformer was destroyed in an explosion. Three men were arrested: a young Aberystwyth University student, Emyr Llywelyn; a Pwllheli businessman named Owain Williams, and a former soldier named John Albert Jones, who was also from Pwllheli. Llywelyn and

Williams received twelve-month jail sentences while Jones was put on probation. Many of those who did time just down the road at Fron-goch would have applauded their action.

The residents of Capel Celyn and their supporters took their protest to the heart of Liverpool and picketed a meeting of the Liverpool Council. When it came to a vote, only one councillor opposed the measure. This was Councillor L. Murphy, who said that, as an Irishman, he knew how the Welsh felt.

Despite all opposition, by 1965 the work had been concluded. The remains of the village of Capel Celyn, with its chapel, cemetery and village school, and a dozen other houses and farms, was submerged under Llyn Celyn's cold, peaty water. The Quaker graveyard where the persecuted ancestors of those who had fled to Pennsylvania in 1862 still lie was also drowned. The lake is two and a half miles long, a mile wide and contains sixteen million gallons of water. It cost £16 million to build and it cost seventy people their homes.

During the opening ceremony on the 21st of October 1965 feelings finally boiled over. Some five hundred protesters ran riot. The microphone wires were cut, which silenced the voices of those dignitaries who had been instrumental in drowning the valley. At that protest, members of the illegal Free Wales Army, who would also attend the fiftieth anniversary of the Rising in Dublin, paraded openly in uniform for the very first time. In 1969, on the day of the Investiture of the English Prince of Wales, four of the members were jailed for periods of between six and eighteen months.

Tryweryn has never been forgotten. Graffiti announcing 'Cofiwch Dryweryn' [Remember Tryweryn] are still to be seen on buildings and rock faces throughout Wales. During exceptionally dry summers the waters retreat far enough to reveal the shame of Wales – and Liverpool – as the remains of some of the ruined houses of Capel Celyn are exposed.

At the height of the project some four hundred people worked on the scheme, which was carried out by surveyors Binney & Deacon and the construction engineers Tarmac. Records show that the official workforce on the 5th of May 1962 was two hundred and ninety-five. Considering the high proportion of Irish labourers who had worked on similar projects, a high percentage of these would also have been Irish. This time they lived in caravans rather than in an oppressive stone building and draughty wooden huts; those caravans were located on the very spot where the North Camp had stood in 1916.

R. J. Lloyd Price, the whisky magnate, would not have been at all surprised by the scheme. As early as 1899 he had written that the Tryweryn river could be dammed in three different places in order to supply water for thirsty Londoners. It is true that the river was dammed in one place only and for the benefit of Liverpool rather than London, but his foresight was remarkable. Had he ventured privately into damming the river and selling water he would probably have been far more successful than he was at distilling and selling whisky.

The Tryweryn dam led to many changes in the valley. The church that stood close to the site of the North Camp was closed and demolished, although the cemetery where seven German soldiers had been buried before being re-interred elsewhere still exists. The church was demolished, not as a result of the dam but because of dwindling congregations, but the dam was responsible for changing the course of the main road. The railway, which had once been so important in the transport of whisky and internees, was closed — not by Transport Minister Lord Beeching's axe, even though that would have been inevitable — but because one stretch of the line would have been drowned by the waters behind the dam. Watcyn L. Jones notes that the last passenger train ran on the 2nd of January 1960, and thereafter the connection between

Bala and Blaenau Ffestiniog which had lasted since 1882 was broken.

A few remains of Fron-goch station have survived – notably the Station House, part of the platform and the signal box. Most of the camp huts have been sold off, but one of the original huts, with a carving of the O'Neill harp on its front, still stands near a local farm, and a solitary hut still occupies a small corner on the site of the North Camp. It is the headquarters of Fron-goch Women's Institute. Some have insisted that it is one of the original huts, the guard house, but that is doubtful. Therefore it seems unlikely that the Institute's anthem 'Jerusalem' is heard in a building where 'A Soldier's Song' would once have been defiantly sung.

The distillery was demolished in 1934. The officers' houses, built originally for the distillery officials and where the camp officers later lived, still stand. Today there is a school where the distillery's tall chimney used to dominate the landscape. Ysgol Bro Tryweryn houses a small exhibition about the distillery and the internment camp. When the school was opened in 1971 there was a call for the classrooms to be named after some of the Irish leaders who had been interned on the site, but events in the Six Counties soon put a stop to that idea.

A thread of irony runs through the long story of Fron-goch, and two more ironies remain. Firstly, during the summer of 2002, a plaque was unveiled by the side of the main road at Fron-goch commemorating those who had been interned nearby. The plaque is in three languages: Welsh, Irish and English, and was funded by the Irish language movement, Conradh na Gaeilge. The branch responsible for its funding was the Liverpool branch, the city that provided a number of Volunteers during the Rising – many of whom, including the Kings and the Kerrs, were unwilling guests at Fron-goch – and the city that was responsible, almost fifty years later, for the drowning of nearby Capel Celyn.

In October 2005, Liverpool City Council apologised for what had been done to Capel Celyn in the name of Liverpool. That apology, coming four decades after the flooding of the closely-knit Welsh community, was widely regarded by the people of the Bala area as an empty and meaningless gesture. It was too little, too late.

Soon after the Fron-goch plaque was unveiled, it was defaced, but it was later cleaned and still stands as a reminder of the seven months in 1916 when a small corner of rural Wales became Irish.

There is another irony. On the 28th of October 2002, Chris Ruane, the Labour MP for Dyffryn Clwyd, spoke in support of the Good Friday Agreement. He mentioned the fact that while his Welsh grandfather Ned Roberts was fighting in the trenches of the Somme in 1916, his Irish grandfather Tom Ruane was an internee at Fron-goch. This was the same Tom Ruane who had lent his plimsolls to de Valera when the Long Fellow escaped from Lincoln Jail in 1919.

Even as this book prepares to go to press, a front-page story in the *Sunday Independent* indicates that the legacy of Fron-goch is still active. The story alleges that eight British soldiers killed during ambushes in Iraq in 2005 were the victims of bombs that were created by the British security services in the early 1990s and passed on to the IRA in what was meant to be a counter-terrorist sting operation. The IRA, having refined the infra-red-activated device, passed the blueprints on to the Palestinians, who in turn passed them on to the Iraqi insurgents. The British Government disclaimed the story and blamed Iran. One or two letters can make a world of difference. For Iran read IRA, and for Basra, read Bala, where it all began ninety years ago.

BIBLIOGRAPHY

Main Sources

Barry, Tom: *Guerilla Days in Ireland*. Anvil Books 1981.

Béaslaí, Piaras: *Michael Collins and the Making of a New Ireland*. 2 vols. Phoenix 1926.

Behan, Brendan: *Brendan Behan's Island*. Bernard Geis 1962.

Bennett, R.: *The Black and Tans*. New English Library 1961.

Breen, Dan: *My Fight for Irish Freedom*. Anvil Books 1964.

Brennan-Whitmore, W. J.: *With the Irish in Frongoch*. Talbot Press, 1917.

–: *Dublin Burning*. Gill & McMillan Ltd 1996.

Coogan, Tim Pat: *Michael Collins: A Biography*. Hutchinson 1990.

Costello, Francis J.: *Enduring the Most*. Brandon Book Publishers 1995.

Cronin, Sean: *Our Own Red Blood*. Muintir Wolf Tone 1966.

Davies, John (Ed.): *Cymru'n Deffro. Hanes y Blaid Genedlaethol 1925-1975*. Y Lolfa 1981.

Deasy, Liam: *Brother Against Brother*. Mercier Press 1998.

de Burca, Séamus: *The Soldier's Song: the Story of Peadar Kearney*. PJ Burke, 1957.

Dwyer, Ryle: *The Squad and the intelligence operations of Michael Collins*. Mercier Press 2005.

Forester, Margery: *Michael Collins: The Lost Leader*. Gill and Macmillan 1971.

Fox, R. M.: *The History of the Irish Citizen Army*. James Duffy & Co 1943.

Gleeson, James: *Bloody Sunday*. First Lyons Press 2004.

Good, Joe. *Enchanted by Dreams: the Journal of a Revolutionary*. Brandon 1996.

Gray, Tony: *Ireland this Century*. Little, Brown and Company 1994.

Hart, Peter: *The IRA and its Enemies*. Oxford University Press 1998.

–: *The IRA at War 1916-1923*. Oxford University Press 2003.

–: *Mick: the Real Michael Collins*. Macmillan 2005.

Inglis, Brian. *Roger Casement* Penguin Books Ltd 2002.

Jones, Thomas: *Whitehall Diary Vol 3, Ireland 1918-1925*. Oxford University Press 1971.

Jones, Watcyn L.: *Cofio Tryweryn*. Gwasg Gomer 1988.

Kee, Robert: *Ireland: A History*. Weidenfeld & Nicholson 1980.

Macardle, Dorothy: *The Irish Republic*. Irish Press 1951.

MacThomáis, Éamonn: *Down Dublin Streets 1916*. Irish Book Bureau 1965

McGuffin, John: *Internment*. Anvil Books 1973

Neeson, Eoin: *The Life and Death of Michael Collins*. Mercier 1968.

O'Brien, Connor Cruise: *Ancestral Voices: Religion and Nationalism in Ireland*. Poolbeg Press 1994

O'Conor, Batt: *With Michael Collins in the Fight for Irish Independence*. Aubane Historical Society 2004.

O'Connor, Frank. *The Big Fellow: Michael Collins and the Irish Revolution*. Clonmore and Reynolds 1965.

O'Connor, M. J.: *Stone Walls . . .* The Dublin Press 1916

O'Connor, Ulick. *Michael Collins and the Troubles: The Struggle for Irish Freedom, 1912 – 1922*. Mainstream Publishing 2001.

O'Kelly, Seán T: *Seán*. Dublin 1963.

O'Leary, Paul (Ed.): *Irish Migrants in Modern Wales*. Liverpool University Press 2004.

O Mahony, Sean: *Frongoch: University of Revolution*. FDR Teoranta 1987.
     –: *Three Murders in Dublin Castle 1916-1921* Elo Publications 2000.
     –: *The First Hunger Strike – Thomas Ashe, 1917*. Elo Publications 2001.

Ó Maoileoin, Séamas: *B'fhiú an Braon Fola*. Sairseal agus Dill 1958.

Parry, Jon: 'The Black Hand: 1916 and Irish Republican Prisoners in North Wales' in Paul O' Leary, ed. *Irish Migrants in Modern Wales*. Liverpool University Press 2004.

Ryan, Annie: *Witnesses: Inside the Easter Rising*. Liberties Press 2005.

Ryan, Desmond: *Michael Collins and the Invisible Army*. Anvil Books 1968.

Shannon, Martin: *Sixteen Roads to Golgotha*. Red Hand Books n.d.

Somerville-Large, Peter: *Irish Voices: Fifty Years of Irish Life 1916-1966*. Chatto and Windus 1999.

Spindler, Karl: *The Mystery of the Casement Ship*. Anvil Books 1965.

Stephens, James: *The Insurrection in Dublin*. Maunsel and Company 1916.

Taber, Robert: *The War of the Flea*. Paladin 1970.

Taylor, Rex: *Michael Collins*. Hutchinson 1958.

Travers, Charles J.: *Seán MacDiarmada (1883-1916)*. Cumann Seanchais Bhreifne 1966

Thomas, Einion Wyn: *Boddi Cwm Tryweryn*. Pecyn Addysgu Archifol. Archifau Gwynedd 1997.

–: *Capel Celyn. Deng Mlynedd o Chwalu: 1955-1965*. Cyhoeddiadau Barddas 1997.

Valiulis, Maryann Gialanella: *Portrait of a Revolutionary: General Richard Mulcahy*. Irish Academic Press 1992.

Weekly Irish Times: *Sinn Féin Rebellion Handbook*. 1917.

Newspaper and magazine sources are noted in the text.

I acknowledge with gratitude the help and support of Einion Wyn Thomas, University of Wales Bangor Archivist, as well as the staff of the National Library of Wales and the Meirionnydd Archives. Dr John Davies, as usual, has been a fountain of knowledge. My thanks to Ioan Roberts for being instrumental in discovering the graves of two Welsh soldiers killed during the Rising. My thanks also to Robin Price of the Rhiwlas Estate for his welcome and geniality. He is, indeed, a gentleman in the true sense of the word. Also thanks to Myrddin ap Dafydd and Gwasg Carreg Gwalch for the usual thoroughness and to Jasmine Donahaye for her meticulous work and valuable advice as editor. Finally, thanks to Sean O Mahony. Without his much-researched volume *Frongoch: University of Revolution* this book would never have seen the light of day.

Acknowledgments

Author: 1, 2, 3, 10, 15, 40, 54, 55, 56, 57, 58, 65, 67, 68, 69, 78

National Library of Wales: 4

Gwynedd Records Office: 9, 12, 13, 14, 39, 45, 46, 47, 48, 63, 64

Price family, Rhiwlas: 6, 7, 8

Gwasg Carreg Gwalch: 5, 16, 17, 18, 19 24, 25, 26, 27, 29, 31, 32, 33, 34, 35, 36, 42, 66, 70, 71, 72, 73, 74, 75, 76, 77, 79, 80, 81, 82, 84, 85, 86, 87, 88, 89

Dublin General Post Office (paintings/photographs on its public walls): 20, 21, 22, 23

Wrth Angor yn Nulyn: 28, 30

National Museum, Ireland: 37, 38, 41, 59, 60

Sean O Mahoney 43, 44, 49, 50, 51, 52, 53

Michael Collins Centre, Castleview, Clonakilty, Co. Cork: 61, 62

Neuadd y Cyfnod, Y Bala: 11, 83 (photo: Gwyn Evans)